STITCH MOUNTAIN

sixth&springbooks NEW YORK

STITCH
MOUNTAIN
30 WARM
KNITS FOR
CONQUERING
THE COLD

LAURA ZANDER

PHOTOGRAPHY BY BRAD SWONETZ

sixth&springbooks 161 Avenue of the Americas, New York, NY 10013   sixthandspringbooks.com

Editorial Director
JOY AQUILINO

Developmental Editor
LISA SILVERMAN

Art Director
DIANE LAMPHRON

Yarn Editor
JOANNA RADOW

Editorial Assistant
JOHANNA LEVY

Instructions Editors
LISA BUCCELLATO
MELINDA MORROW
SANDI PROSSER

Technical Illustrations
ULI MONCH

Photography
BRAD SWONETZ

Fashion Stylist
ANNA COHEN

Hair and Makeup
EDIN CARPENTER

Vice President
TRISHA MALCOLM

Publisher
CARRIE KILMER

Production Manager
DAVID JOINNIDES

President
ART JOINNIDES

Chairman
JAY STEIN

Library of Congress Cataloging-in-Publication Data

Zander, Laura.
Stitch mountain : 30 warm knits for conquering the cold / Laura Zander.
     pages cm
ISBN: 978-1-936096-67-1 (hardback)
1. Knitting—Patterns. 2. Cold weather clothing. I. Title.
TT825.Z37 2013
746.43'2—dc23
                                    2013031762

MANUFACTURED IN CHINA

1 3 5 7 9 10 8 6 4 2

First Edition

STITCH MOUNTAIN

TO THE
    SKI HEROES
OF MY LIFE,
    DOUG AND HUCK.

❋CONTENTS

PAGE 26

PAGE 29

PAGE 47

PAGE 44

PAGE 50

PAGE 66

PAGE 71

PAGE 87

PAGE 81

PAGE 84

PAGE 76

PAGE 94

PAGE 91

PAGE 99

PAGE 102

PAGE 119

PAGE 122

PAGE 129

PAGE 105

PAGE 111

PAGE 115

PAGE 132

PAGE 135

My involvement with *Stitch Mountain* was one part serendipity and two parts chance.

I first met Laura and Doug Zander a few years ago, when I was hired to photograph Jimmy Beans Wool for an article in *Fortune Small Business*. We hit it off and spent a lot of time talking about the outdoors and skiing. After the shoot, I went back to San Diego, which I now call home and where photography and surfing make up the better part of my day.

So what's a Southern California guy like me doing photographing a knitting book? The reason is simple: I love to knit! I've been hooked since age 23, when I learned from my grandmother while living in L.A. From hats and beer cozies to iPod cases and scarves, I'm always surprised what you can turn out with a ball of yarn and some time. When Laura called me out of the blue to ask if I would be the photographer for this book, I jumped at the opportunity. Besides, it's not every day you're asked to photograph knitted gear in the snow!

It was super-exciting to photograph a book that combines my three favorite things: winter sports, knitting, and photography. For me, knitting is a meditative sport; I feel the same way when I'm surfing, taking pictures, or snowboarding: a complete sense of focus and exhilaration. A book about passion and craft, *Stitch Mountain* explores the awesome world of winter sports, yarn, and the contagious need for speed. From the moonlit shots in the snow to the iconic handknitted winter gear, I hope you enjoy this book as much as I loved capturing it, and that it inspires you to express your own artistic passions, on and off the slopes. ❄

✳ A Message from the U.S. Ski and Snowboard Association

Skiing and snowboarding are more than sports—they are a lifestyle. Fashion, art, and style are the fiber of winter sports and an integral part of the lives of skiers and snowboarders.

As America's Olympic sports organization for skiing and snowboarding, the U.S. Ski and Snowboard Association is proud to partner with Jimmy Beans Wool and Red Heart. *Stitch Mountain* is an amazing collection of tales tracing the history of America's greatest ski and snowboarding stars with the evolution of knitted winter gear—a key part of the sports' style.

While the stars are known for their speed and agility on the mountain, their passion truly lies in the winter lifestyle. It's about style—on the mountain and off. It's about athletes like Olympic medalist and X Games champion Lindsey Jacobellis, who finds comfort and a sense of accomplishment in being skilled at a craft like knitting, and teaching others through her efforts with Hats 4 Hounds.

Thanks, Jimmy Beans Wool and Red Heart, for being a part of our sports' lifestyle and bringing *Stitch Mountain* to us. ✳

My husband and I started our business, Jimmy Beans Wool, in 2002 because we love to ski. Well, I love to ski. Doug *lives* to ski.

In 2001, we moved from the Bay Area to the ski town of Truckee, California. We wanted to live in the mountains to be closer to activities we loved, like skiing, hiking, and biking—but we had no idea how we were going to make a living. As luck would have it, I love knitting, too, and Truckee needed a yarn shop. So we opened Jimmy Beans Wool, and quickly realized that our two passions (mine: knitting; his: skiing) were more intertwined than we had imagined. In retrospect, it seems obvious: people knit when it's cold, and skiers need warm gear out in the cold!

We saw firsthand the relationship among knitting, knitwear, and winter sports. Athletes would come into the shop looking to knit custom gear, either to show their style on the hill or just to keep warm. And it wasn't only recreational athletes—the pros came in, too!

In 2011 we became a sponsor of U.S. Snowboarding and Freeskiing, in collaboration with Red Heart yarns. Through this sponsorship—and our years living in the mountains and skiing at one of the world's best hills, Squaw Valley—we met world-class skiers and snowboarders, which got us thinking: What better way to show the connection between knitwear and winter sports than through the stories of some of the best, most inspirational athletes in the world? Thus, *Stitch Mountain* was born.

I asked a few athletes what they thought of a book geared toward knitting your own ski and snowboard gear, and the response was overwhelmingly positive. In fact, when I approached Debbie Armstrong and Edie Thys Morgan—both Olympians *and* knitters—with the idea, they couldn't believe no one had written this book before. Knitting was an integral part of their skiing and racing lives, as you'll learn from Edie's essay in the back of the book. We've been amazed at the number of athletes who knit or crochet! Of course, not all the athletes profiled in this book knit, but every one understands and appreciates the value of a good hat, scarf, and set of mittens.

So, knitters of all skill levels (and athletic abilities), we invite you to share in the stories of these amazing athletes and to create your own cold-weather gear!

A PERFECT MATCH
※ Knitting and Winter Sports

Knitting and winter sports have histories as intertwined as an intricate cable pattern. Knitting helped to create sportswear as we know it. We take our athletic gear for granted, but the origins of snow sports and the knitted fashions worn while pursuing them are fascinating.

Knitted garments have been made for thousands of years. People have been using skis, skates, and sleds for wintertime transportation—and undoubtedly entertainment—for millennia as well. By the middle of the nineteenth century, people began to organize these methods of winter travel into sports and competition.

As races and games became the main purpose for skating, skiing, and sledding, competitors dressed for the occasion. Few if any of the early athletes had clothes specifically for their cold-weather sports. Rather, they chose the clothes they owned that best provided warmth and allowed mobility without undue bulk or weight. Knitted clothing was ideal for these emerging needs.

Sportswear based on knitted fabric was both practical and decorative. The most commonly available fiber by far was wool, and knitted wool kept athletes warm in snowy and icy environments. Knitted fabric is elastic, so garments could be made to fit and have enough give so they stretched as the racer moved, then sprang back to the original shape. And knitting was already a tradition in the places snow sports were developing. Handknit garments become integral to outfitting early skiers, skaters, and other winter athletes.

Costumes for early skiers offered so many opportunities for knitters! Hats, scarves, sweaters, mittens, leggings, stockings, and socks could all be knitted by hand.

HEADGEAR
A knitted hat had to stay on throughout a race, and basic beanies were—and still are—an ideal head covering for skiers. But why stop with a plain beanie? The hat might have Fair Isle designs, cables, or almost any colorwork or texture. In the 1950s this basic hat became a skiing classic when Ma Moriarty started producing them commercially in Stowe, Vermont. Beanies or stocking caps have undergone design transformations in recent decades: hats are outrageously long, often with wide stripes; or adorned with two large pompoms at the crown, resembling the ears on a stuffed animal. They lost their crowns and became headbands to warm the ears. Or their crowns were extended and made slouchy. They have taken on earflaps with long cords and tassels, chulla style. Stocking caps are relatively small and easy to knit, and knitters have added a splash of fun and color, even using neon-colored yarn. Balaclavas or ski masks were knitted to keep skiers' heads and faces warm in frigid weather; sadly, this heavy-duty head covering has become less desirable on the slopes, though the milder neck gaiter is entirely acceptable.

SWEATERS
Ski sweaters were often the outermost layer worn—not covered by a parka—and knitters in different regions developed particular ways to make their sweaters. Ribs and cables give extra elasticity. Norwegian and Icelandic pullovers use multiple colors in rich patterns, and multiple strands of yarn make a sweater warmer. The Austrians who established alpine ski schools in the U.S. from the 1930s onward wore colorful, allover Fair-Isle sweaters, sweaters so beautiful that knitters took up their needles to achieve the same colorful effects. Reflecting the Nordic tradition, Dale of Norway has outfitted the Norwegian Olympic team first in 1956 and in every games since; the company began publishing knitting patterns in the 1960s so knitters could produce their own medal-worthy sweaters and more.

HANDS
Mittens and knitted gloves were important for keeping hands warm. They are relatively small and allow the knitter to experiment with patterns. Felted wool makes even more effective mittens, blocking wind and water and keeping the skier warm.

FEET
Knitted socks, stockings, and leggings were essential to skiers and other winter athletes. They reached their pinnacle in the traditional gear worn by Nordic skiers, where the outer layer of stocking reached the

knee and featured intricate geometric patterns. A well-turned-out Norwegian setting out to ski all day would have hat, sweater, mittens, and stockings all knit in the same color scheme, with coordinated patterns from the Selbu district—a tour-de-force of handknitting! Only the knickerbockers would be made from woven wool, quite possibly hand-woven.

American skiers were wearing their largely knitted sportswear to train and to race from the 1880s onward. In 1924, when the Winter Olympics were separated from the Olympics taking place in the summer, Americans won 4 of the 49 medals. Eight years later the United States hosted the Winter Olympics for the first time, in Lake Placid, New York. The Winter Games have taken place in the United States three times since: in 1960 in Squaw Valley, 1980 in Lake Placid again, and 2002 in Salt Lake City.

Through the twentieth century, Americans had more opportunities to ski as resorts were developed. In the 1930s, Alpine-style resorts developed in New England and Idaho, with ski schools led by talented Austrians and others who learned to ski on the Alps. After World War II more resorts opened, at Aspen Mountain and elsewhere. With better facilities came more serious programs to train and develop

athletes. The achievements of American skiers, snowboarders, and other winter athletes are apparent in medal tables.

What skiers now wear for competition has become as sophisticated and technical as the equipment they use. Handknits are rarely part of their racing gear, other than the occasional knitted beanie. Recreational skiers may wear more of the handknit sweaters that are part of the traditions of skiing.

All skiers, competitors and enthusiasts alike, can bring out their handknits for "après ski," a term that literally means "after skiing." It describes not just a time of day but a mood and frame of mind. When runs and laps are over for the day, skiers shift to the fun of socializing in lodges, restaurants, and bars. "Après ski" was coined in the 1950s, and the term and culture took root quickly. Handknit garments and accessories take center stage once there are no requirements to resist wind, keep ultra warm and dry, or give the athlete a millisecond advantage. Now a skier can wear a silk tunic, a draped scarf, or any other garment that looks fun. Après skiwear need not fit closely, repel water, warm the wearer, or perform in any other serious way. The best way to define après ski? An excuse to show off beautiful handknits! ❋

PAGE 132

PAGE 135

PAGE 122

PAGE 76

CLOSE KNIT

✳ BY OLYMPIAN EDIE THYS MORGAN

The life of a professional winter athlete is not always glamorous. Yes, it means going to beautiful places in pursuit of a sport you love. But those places are often obscure, remote, and hard to reach. Constant travel is part of the deal. As a member of the U.S. Ski Team, I knew this life well. It wasn't so long ago that we didn't have iPods and cell phones and computers. Instead of GPS we used well-worn and often outdated road maps; instead of YouTube we had a few VHS tapes that we watched until we knew each line by heart; instead of email we had the postal service and lots of patience. And when we were thinking of someone special, we didn't send a text—we knit a hat.

We knit in vans, on planes, and in hotel rooms. We knit on layovers in airports, in lodges between runs, and during long team meetings. As one of my teammates put it, "What else do you do on the Black Tongue Route [the long, Alp-spanning stretch of Autobahn across northern Italy, so called because of all the coffee one typically drank to stay awake en route], or that cross-country trip when we ran out of gas at two a.m. in Iowa?" A few had been taught by their mothers and grandmothers, but most of us learned from more seasoned teammates, and in that way the tradition passed down, weaving one generation into the next. We knit for our crushes du jour, personalizing their hats with their names, initials, or a special message on the inside fold. One friend, after knitting a hat for a particularly coveted boyfriend, admitted, "I must have ripped out the bottom of that hat half a dozen times before I got the words right."

It wasn't only girls—some of the most prolific and creative knitters were the Alpha guys. And it certainly wasn't all about romance. We knit hats for all friends and all occasions, but most often for good luck. My teammate Chantal, whose coach, Deb, had knit her a good-luck hat in advance of her first World Cup, stayed up all night to knit a good-luck hat for Diann in time for her first World Championships. Even though she was just seventeen, Diann won a gold medal there.

Most of us started with the classic three-point Moriarty design (which inspired the Snowflake Hat, below; see page 115), made popular by the skiing family from Stowe. Regional differences in style were evident, with easterners gravitating toward thick lopi wool ideal for Arctic temps, and westerners opting for thinner, lightweight fibers. Once the basic technique was mastered, people embellished their creations with pompoms and tassels, bows, ribbons, or charms. My sister once got offered a tidy sum of Swiss francs in a European lift line for her hat that featured a seaside scene with sewn-on sea creatures and beach toys. She sold it on the spot, of course. The best knitters had a backlog of orders, and offered a customized choice of colors and designs.

❄ CLOSE KNIT

Production increased dramatically with the emergence of quick-to-make beanies and headbands.

Knitting initiated boundless creativity, with designs ranging from simple flecks of color to repeating geometric patterns to intricate scenes and animals. True masters, like Tamara McKinney's sister Ouisha ("Ouisha Hats" were the Holy Grail), crafted elaborate scenes with horses, fluffy angora bunnies, and even desert landscapes complete with cactuses and howling coyotes.

I know for sure that knitting was and is good for us, though I can't begin to count the ways. Some claim that knitting gets you into a flow state, where you lose the "judgmental mind." Admittedly, like a runner's high, it can become an addiction. One teammate confessed that it took her an extra term to get through high school, largely because of the time she spent doodling knitwear designs and mapping out charted patterns on graph paper.

Part time-killer, part creative outlet, part stress-reliever, knitting became, more than anything, our way of connecting with one another and with friends and family far away. The process itself—coming up with concepts and designs just right for each person or situation, and sharing the progress—is social. For the giver, it represents time spent focusing on something and someone else. For the receiver, it is a tangible reminder of the creator's thoughtfulness and effort. Wear anything knit just for you and you can't help but smile, even at its imperfections. The missed stitch, the sudden change of color, the slight irregularities of gauge and design, all hint at the knitter's personality, desperation for material, and state of mind.

I recently interviewed Betsy Clifford, a Canadian world champion alpine racer who had been a good friend of Annemarie Moser Proell, the winningest female ski racer of all time. Clifford's most vivid memories of Annemarie were not of the steely competitor, but of the fun-loving girl who taught her how to knit. Neither spoke the other's language all that well, yet I could just see them together, world-class archrivals, knitting and laughing like best friends.

There is something timeless and precious about the power of knitting, and I am heartened to see that its pursuit and creations are appreciated as much as ever. Sure, times have changed, but the urge to create and connect, to be bound by a common thread, will never disappear. Who knows? Someday you may get a text from someone you love who is in a cold, faraway land, typing away comfortably in the fingerless gloves you knit. ❄

PEAK MOMENTS IN U.S. WINTER SPORTS

❋ Highlights in skiing and snowboarding

1882

Nansen Ski Club, the first organized skiing club in the U.S., is formed in Berlin, New Hampshire.

1905

The National Ski Association, which has since become the U.S. Ski and Snowboard Association, is formed in Ishpeming, Michigan.

1924

Inaugural Winter Olympics, in Chamonix, France. Some winter sports have been included in the Olympic Games since 1908. The events are Nordic and exclusively for men. U.S. athletes win 4 of the 49 medals.

1932

For the first time, the U.S. hosts a major international skiing competition: the Winter Olympics in Lake Placid, New York.

1933

The U.S. Civilian Conservation Corps cuts trails on Mount Mansfield in Vermont, leading to the development of a ski resort in Stowe and the rapid growth of Alpine skiing in New England. Alpine skiing resorts begin in the west with Sun Valley, Idaho.

1936

The Winter Olympics in Garmisch-Partenkirchen, Germany, include Alpine events for the first time. Another first: events for female skiers.

1948

At the Winter Olympics in St. Moritz, Switzerland, Gretchen Fraser (in a sweater and woolen pants) wins gold in the slalom and silver in the combined—the first Alpine medals for an American athlete.

1956

The Winter Olympics in Cortina D'Ampezzo, Italy, are televised for the first time, and the Moriarty hat debuts in Stowe, Vermont. Olympians and many other skiers continue to buy them through 2006, and vintage Moriarties are still coveted.

1960

The United States hosts the Winter Olympics in Squaw Valley, California.

1964

In Innsbruck, American men win Olympic medals in Alpine skiing for the first time: Billy Kidd, wearing a Moriarty hat, takes silver, and Jimmie Heuga wins bronze, in the slalom.

1976

Bill Koch wins silver in the 30-kilometer cross-country skiing event at the Winter Olympics in Innsbruck, the first American to win an Olympic medal for Nordic skiing.

1980

The U.S. once again hosts the Winter Olympics when it returns to Lake Placid.

1992

Jeff Hamilton wins a bronze medal in speed skiing at the Winter Olympics in Albertville, France. Hamilton is the first to reach 150 miles per hour on skis.

1998

In Nagano, Japan, snowboarding is included in the Winter Olympics for the first time. American Picabo Street wins gold in the super-G.

2002

The U.S. hosts the Winter Olympics in Salt Lake City, Utah. Americans Vonetta Flowers and Jill Bakken win gold in the first Olympic bobsled event to include women. Flowers is the first black person to win a gold medal in any Winter Olympic event.

2006

American snowboarders dominate the medal tally at the Winter Olympics in Turin, Italy, with Hannah Teter, Shaun White, and Seth Wescott winning gold.

2010

Lindsey Vonn wins gold and silver at the Winter Olympics in Vancouver, Canada. She is now the most decorated American skier in history—and is often spotted sporting a knit beanie.

*THE PROJECTS

DESIGNED BY GWEN BORTNER

DOUBLE-KNIT COWL

Double the fun and double the warmth with a playful cowl knit in a luscious mohair/silk blend.

 Inspired by X Games champion freestyle skier MADDIE BOWMAN

SIZE
Instructions are written for one size.

KNITTED MEASUREMENTS
• *Circumference*
Approx 20"/51cm

• *Height*
Approx 5½"/14cm

MATERIALS
1 .88oz/25g ball (each approx 229yd/210m) of Rowan *Kidsilk Haze* (mohair/silk) in #634 cream (A)

1 1¾oz/50g ball (each approx 460yd/420m) of Rowan *Kidsilk Haze Stripe* (mohair/silk) in #205 circus (B)

Size 5 (3.75mm) circular needle, 20"/51 cm long, *or size to obtain gauge*

Stitch markers

Tapestry needle

GAUGE
18 sts and 32 rnds = 4"/10cm over one knitted side of chart pat with yarns held double using size 5 (3.75mm) needle.
Take time to check gauge.

NOTE
One square on the chart represents 2 sts, 1 front st and 1 back st. Cowl will have charted pattern on front and back, colors reversed. Cowl is worked with yarns held double throughout.

STITCH GLOSSARY
FA With both colors held to back, k front st with A; with both colors held to front, p back st with B.
FB With both colors held to back, k front st with B; with both colors held to front, p back st with A.

COWL
With both yarns held double, *[cast on 1 st with A, cast on 1 st with B] 30 times, place marker (pm); rep from * twice more—90 sts each color, 180 sts total. Join to work in the rnd, being careful not to twist sts, pm for beg of rnd.

BEG CHART
RND 1 Work 30-st rep 3 times around, slipping markers. Mark this side as front of cowl. Cont in chart pat until rnd 30 has been worked once, then rep rnds 1–13 once more.
NEXT RND With both colors held to back, k front st with A; with both colors held to front, p back st with B.
BIND-OFF RND Sl 1 st purlwise, *sl 1 st purlwise, pass first slipped st over second slipped st; rep from * until 2 sts rem.

FINISHING
Break yarn, leaving 10"/25.5cm tail. Thread tail through rem sts to secure. Block lightly to measurements. ❋

❋DOUBLE-KNIT COWL

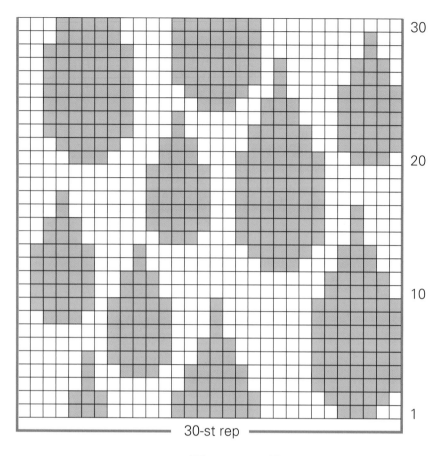

30-st rep

COLOR KEY □ Cream ■ Circus (B)

MADDIE BOWMAN
This white cowl sprinkled with colorful balloons is inspired by Maddie's perspective on her favorite sport: "I think skiing should always be for fun, like a party!"

In 2012, Maddie Bowman had a pretty epic senior year in high school. After playing on the South Lake Tahoe High School girls' state champion soccer team, she podiumed in nearly every major freeskiing event. She scored invitations to the Dew Tour and the X Games, taking home a gold and a silver, respectively, and finished the season by winning the AFP World Championship halfpipe event. Nice graduation present! In 2013 Maddie scored World Cup and X Games gold, showing she's still riding the learning curve. Her ski racer parents got her on skis at age two, and she rocketed through all the ski programs at Sierra-at-Tahoe before falling in love with freeskiing. Maddie also loves mountain biking, hiking, wakeboarding, backpacking, and, of course, beaching it. "I try to live a really active life and am easily bored when I have too much down time."

STRIPED-SLEEVE SWEATER

A zippered mock neck and double stripes down each arm add up to simply sporty style.

 Inspired by Olympic speed skiing medalist JEFF HAMILTON

SIZES

Instructions are written for unisex size X-Small. Changes for Small, Medium, Large, X-Large, and XX-Large are in parentheses. (Shown in size Medium.)

KNITTED MEASUREMENTS

- *Chest* 36½ (40, 42½, 45½, 49½, 53½)"/92.5 (101.5, 108, 115.5, 125.5, 136)cm

- *Length* 25 (25¾, 26½, 27½, 28½, 29½)"/63.5 (65.5, 67.5, 70, 71, 75)cm

- *Upper arm* 14½ (16, 17, 18, 19, 21)"/39.5 (37, 43, 45.5, 48, 53.5)cm

MATERIALS

4 (4, 4, 5, 5, 6) 7oz/198g skeins (each approx 364yd/333m) of Red Heart *Super Saver Economy* (acrylic) in #886 blue (MC) **4**

1 skein in #316 soft white (CC)

One each sizes 7 and 9 (4.5 and 5.5mm) circular needle, 32"/80cm long, *or size to obtain gauge*

One pair each sizes 7 and 9 (4.5 and 5.5mm) needles

Stitch markers

Stitch holders or scrap yarn

1 non-separating zipper, 7"/18cm long

GAUGE

16 sts and 21 rows = 4"/10cm over St st using size 9 (5.5mm) needles. *Take time to check gauge.*

STITCH GLOSSARY

KFB Knit into the front and back of next st—1 st increased.

K1, P1 RIB

(over an even number of sts)
ROW/RND 1 (RS) *K1, p1; rep from * to end.
Rep row/rnd 1 for k1, p1 rib.

NOTES

1) Sweater is worked from the neck edge down. When yoke is complete, body is joined in one piece and worked in rnds.
2) The collar is picked up later and knit. Sleeves are worked back and forth and seamed.

BODY

With larger circular needle and MC, cast on 48 (50, 52, 54, 56, 58) sts. Do not join.
ROW 1 (RS) With MC, k1, kfb (left front), place marker (pm), with MC, kfb; with CC, k2; with MC, k4; with CC, k2; with MC, kfb (left sleeve), pm, with MC, kfb, k22 (24, 26, 28, 30, 32), kfb (back), pm, with MC, kfb;

with CC, k2; with MC, k4; with CC, k2; with MC, kfb (right sleeve), pm, with MC, kfb, k1 (right front)—56 (58, 60, 62, 64, 66) sts.
ROW 2 (WS) With MC, p3, slip marker (sm), with MC, p2; with CC, p2; with MC, p4; with CC, p2; with MC, p2; sm, with MC, p26 (28, 30, 32, 34, 36), sm, with MC, p2; with CC, p2; with MC, p4; with CC, p2; with MC, p2, sm, with MC, p3.

✳STRIPED-SLEEVE SWEATER

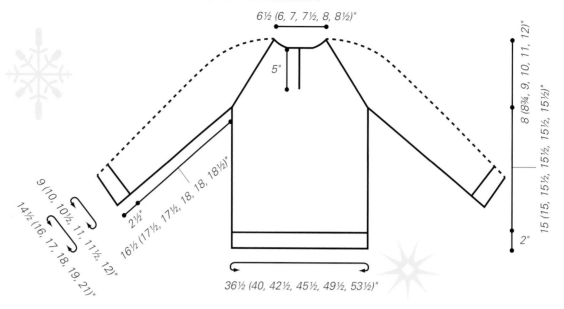

6½ (6, 7, 7½, 8, 8½)"

5"

8 (8¾, 9, 10, 11, 12)"

15 (15, 15½, 15½, 15½, 15½)"

2"

9 (10, 10½, 11, 11½, 12)"

14½ (16, 17, 18, 19, 21)"

2½"

16½ (17½, 17½, 18, 18, 18½)"

36½ (40, 42½, 45½, 49½, 53½)"

Keeping continuity of color pat as now established, proceed as foll:
ROW 3 K1, M1, *knit to 1 st before 1st marker, kfb, sm, kfb; rep from * 3 times more, knit to last st, M1, k1—66 (68, 70, 72, 74, 76) sts.
ROW 4 Work in pat to end of row, slipping markers.
Rep last 2 rows 1 (1, 1, 2, 2, 2) times

more, end with a WS row—76 (78, 80, 92, 94, 96) sts.
NEXT ROW (RS) K1, M1, *knit to 1 st before next marker, kfb, sm, kfb; rep from * 3 times more, knit to last st, M1, k1, turn, cast on 8 (8, 10, 10, 11, 12) sts—94 (96, 100, 112, 115, 118) sts.
NEXT ROW (WS) Work in pat to end of row, turn, cast on 8 (8, 10, 10, 11, 12) sts—102 (104, 110, 122, 126, 130) sts.
NEXT ROW (RS) *Knit to 1 st before 1st marker, kfb, sm, kfb; rep from * 3 times more, knit to end of row—110 (112, 118, 130, 134, 138) sts.
NEXT ROW (WS) Work in pat to end of row, slipping markers.
Rep last 2 rows, inc 8 sts every RS row, 7 times more, then rep first row once, end with RS row.
NEXT (JOINING) RND (RS) Cast on 1 st, join to beg of row and knit to end of rnd, pm.
NEXT RND *Knit to 1 st before next marker, kfb, sm, kfb; rep from * 3 times more, knit to end of rnd—175 (177, 183, 195, 199, 203) sts.
NEXT RND Work in pat to end of rnd, slipping markers.

Rep last 2 rnds, inc 8 sts every other rnd, 8 (10, 11, 12, 15, 17) times, end with a rnd worked even—239 (257, 271, 291, 319, 339) sts.

DIVIDE FOR BODY AND SLEEVES
NEXT ROW (RS) Knit to first marker, remove marker, sl next 52 (56, 58, 62, 66, 72) sts onto holder for left sleeve, cast on 6 (8, 8, 10, 10, 12) sts (left underarm), remove marker, k66 (72, 76, 82, 90, 96), remove marker, sl next 52 (56, 58, 62, 66, 72) sts onto holder for right sleeve, cast on 6 (8, 8, 10, 10, 12) sts (right underarm), remove marker, knit to end of row—147 (161, 171, 183, 199, 215) sts. Do not turn.
Cont working in rnds until piece measures 15 (15, 15½, 15½, 15½, 15½)"/38 (38, 39.5, 39.5, 39.5, 39.5)cm from joining rnd, dec 1 st at center back—146 (160, 170, 182, 198, 214) sts.
Change to smaller circular needle and work in k1, p1 rib for 2"/5cm. Bind off in rib.

❄STRIPED-SLEEVE SWEATER

JEFF HAMILTON
The stripes on Jeff's sweater echo the straight tracks his skis make as they speed down the mountain.

SLEEVES
With larger straight needles, sl 52 (56, 58, 62, 66, 72) sts from holder onto needles, ready for a RS row. With MC, cast on 3 (4, 5, 5, 5, 6) sts at beg of next 2 rows—58 (64, 68, 72, 76, 84) sts. Do not join. Working back and forth in rows and keeping continuity of vertical stripes, work in St st, decreasing 1 st at each end of 5th and every following 6th (6th, 6th, 6th, 4th, 4th) row 5 (4, 10, 13, 2, 9) times, then every 8th (8th, 8th, 6th, 6th, 6th) row 5 (7, 2, 0, 12, 8) times—36 (40, 42, 44, 46, 48) sts. Work even until sleeve measures 16½ (17½, 17½, 18, 18, 18½)"/42 (44.5, 44.5, 45.5, 45.5, 47)cm from underarm cast-on, end with a WS row.

Change to smaller needles and work in k1, p1 rib for 2½"/6.5cm, end with a WS row.
Bind off in rib.

FINISHING
Sew sleeve seams. Sew sleeve underarm to body underarm.

COLLAR
With smaller circular needle, RS facing and MC, pick up and k 70 (74, 78, 84, 86, 90) sts evenly along neck opening. Do not join. Work in k1, p1 rib for 2½"/6.5cm, end with a WS row. Bind off in rib.
Sew zipper to collar/center front opening.❄

When Jeff Hamilton was a kid, he spent hours in his bedroom practicing his tuck. The early aerodynamics training paid off: when speed skiing debuted in the 1992 Winter Olympics, Hamilton and his tuck were there to win bronze. "Speed skiing is basically drag racing," Jeff explains. "Zero to one-fifty in about fifteen seconds." The four-time World Speed Skiing Champion was the first person to break 150 mph on skis. Jeff also holds a more painful record: the fastest crash (151 mph) in a nonmotorized sport. It included six football fields of sliding, the first taking two seconds. Ow! Jeff escaped with relatively minor injuries and can still be found on the slopes of Tahoe's Squaw Valley, where he is a managing broker of Sierra Sotheby's International Realty, and Sugar Bowl, where his daughters, Eleanore and Frances, are on the ski team. Jeff and his wife, Carolyn, live in Truckee, California.

DESIGNED BY RACHEL RODEN

TWISTED-STITCH MITTS

A warm wool knits up into a fun pair of mitts with pinstripes and a winding twisted-stitch motif.

 Inspired by Olympic alpine skier MARCO SULLIVAN

SIZE
Instructions are written for women's size Small. Changes for Large are in parentheses.

KNITTED MEASUREMENTS
• *Hand circumference*
  7 (8)"/18 (20.5)cm

• *Length*
  7½"/19cm

MATERIALS
1 1¾oz/50g ball (each approx 174yd/160m) of Rowan *Pure Wool 4 Ply* (superwash wool) each in #421 glade (A), #451 porcelaine (B), and #419 avocado (C) 〔1〕

One set (5) size 2 (2.75mm) double-pointed needles (dpns) *or size to obtain gauge*

Stitch markers

Small amount of scrap yarn

GAUGE
28 sts and 56 rows = 4"/10cm over garter stitch using size 2 (2.75mm) needles.
Take time to check gauge.

STITCH GLOSSARY
LT Knit 2nd st tbl, do not slip off needle, knit 1st st, slip both sts off needle.
RT K2tog, do not slip off needle, knit 1st st, slip both sts off needle.

CORRUGATED RIB
(over an even number of sts)
RND 1 *With B, k1; with A, p1; rep

from * to end of rnd.
Rep rnd 1 for corrugated rib.

GARTER STRIPE PATTERN
RND 1 With A, knit.
RND 2 With A, purl.
RND 3 With B, knit.
RND 4 With B, purl.
Rep these 4 rnds for garter stripe pat.

NOTE
When working chart, slip stitches purlwise wyib.

LEFT MITT

CUFF

With A, cast on 50 (58) sts and divide evenly over 4 dpns. Join to work in the rnd, being careful not to twist sts, and place marker (pm) for beg of rnd. Work 10 rnds in corrugated rib.

BODY

RND 1 With A, k6 (8), work rnd 1 of chart over next 16 sts, with A, knit to end of rnd—51 (59) sts.
RND 2 With A, p6 (8), work rnd 2 of chart over next 17 sts, purl to end of rnd.
RND 3 With B, k6 (8), work rnd 3 of chart over next 17 sts, knit to end of rnd.
RND 4 With B, p6 (8), work rnd 4 of chart over next 17 sts, purl to end of rnd.
Cont in pat as established, alternating A and B every 2 rnds, until end of chart.

THUMB GUSSET

RND 47 With B, k6 (8), work rnd 3 of chart over next 17 sts, knit to last st, pm, M1, k1, M1—53 (61) sts.
RND 48 With B, p6 (8), work rnd 4 of chart over next 17 sts, purl to end of rnd.
RND 49 With A, k6 (8), work rnd 5 of chart over next 17 sts, knit to marker, M1, k3, M1—55 (63) sts.
RND 50 With A, p6 (8), work rnd 6 of chart over next 17 sts, purl to end of rnd.
Cont as now est, alternating A and B every 2 rnds and inc 2 sts every other rnd until there are 15 (17) sts in thumb gusset, end with a purl rnd.

NEXT RND Work in pat to marker, place next 15 (17) sts on scrap yarn, cast on 1 st, join to beg of rnd—50 (58) sts. Cont in pat to end of chart.

TOP EDGE

Work 6 rnds in corrugated rib. Break B. With A, bind off in rib.

THUMB

Place 15 (17) sts of thumb onto 3 dpns. Attach the working yarn in the color to continue garter stripe pat.
RND 1 K15 (17), with 4th dpn, pick up and k 3 sts at base of thumb—18 (20) sts. Distribute sts evenly over 4 dpns. Work a further 6 rnds of garter stripe pat.
Work 4 rnds in corrugated rib. Break B. With A, bind off in rib.

RIGHT MITT

CUFF

With A, cast on 50 (58) sts and divide evenly over 4 dpns. Join to work in the rnd, being careful not to twist sts, and pm for beg of rnd. Work 10 rnds in corrugated rib.

BODY

RND 1 With A, k28 (34), work rnd 1 of chart over next 16 sts, knit to end of rnd—51 (59) sts.
RND 2 With A, p28 (34), work rnd 2 of chart over next 17 sts, purl to end of rnd.
RND 3 With B, k28 (34), work rnd 3 of chart over next 17 sts, with B, knit to end of rnd.
RND 4 With B, p28 (34), work rnd 4 of chart over next 17 sts, with B, purl to end of rnd.
Cont in pat as established, alternating A and B every 2 rnds, until end of chart.

THUMB GUSSET

RND 47 With B, M1, k1, M1, pm, k27 (33), work rnd 3 of chart over next 17 sts, knit to last st—53 (61) sts.
RND 48 With B, p30 (36), work rnd 4 of chart over next 17 sts, purl to end of rnd.
RND 49 With A, M1, k3, M1, k27 (33), work rnd 5 of chart over next 17 sts, knit to marker—55 (63) sts.
RND 50 With A, p32 (38), work rnd 6 of chart over next 17 sts, purl to end of rnd.
Cont as now est, alternating A and B every 2 rnds and inc 2 sts every other rnd until there are 15 (17) sts in thumb gusset, end with a purl rnd.
NEXT RND Place first 15 (17) sts on scrap yarn, cast on 1 st, work in pat to end of rnd—50 (58) sts. Cont in pat to end of chart.

TOP EDGE

Work 6 rnds in corrugated rib. Break B. With A, bind off in rib.

THUMB

Place 15 (17) sts of thumb onto 3 dpns. Attach the working yarn in the color to continue garter stripe pat.
RND 1 K15 (17), with 4th dpn, pick up and k 3 sts at base of thumb—18 (20) sts. Distribute sts evenly over 4 dpns. Work a further 6 rnds of garter stripe pat.
Work 4 rnds in corrugated rib. Break B. With A, bind off in rib.

FINISHING

Optional: With C, embroider "Marco Rocks," or your own phrase, on top edge, using chain stitch. Block to measurements. ❋

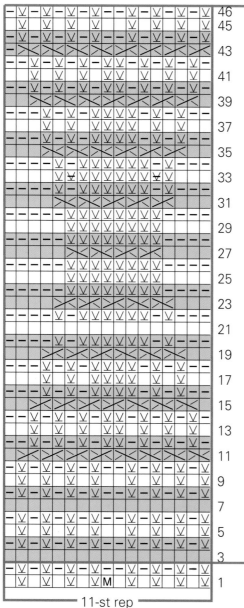

COLOR AND STITCH KEY

- ☐ Knit
- ⊟ Purl
- ⊻ Sl 1 purlwise wyib
- Ⓜ M1
- ⧅ RT
- ⧄ LT
- ▧ Glade (A)
- ☐ Porcelaine (B)

rep
rows 3–46

11-st rep

MARCO SULLIVAN

You can't hold your cowbells if your hands are cold, so you might want to have a pair of these mittens, with their undeniable "Marco Rocks" message.

Want to spot the Marco Sullivan fans in the stands at a World Cup downhill finish? Just look for a sea of green "Marco Rocks" hats. Tahoe born and bred, Marco started skiing on a snow-covered gravel hill in his backyard at age three and graduated to Squaw's Mighty Mite program. Squaw's gnarly terrain made Marco a four-event skier, but in 2001 he decided to specialize in speed. A year later he competed in Salt Lake City at the 2002 Olympics. In 2006 Marco made his second Olympic team and won his first World Cup downhill. In 2009 he placed third in Switzerland's grueling Lauberhorn downhill. Lately, the easygoing mountain man has mixed things up, making films in Alaska and Helsinki and becoming a three-time "Arctic Man" champ. Last season Marco was back on the World Cup podium, reminding us that he does, indeed, rock.

DESIGNED BY GWEN BORTNER

DOUBLE-LAYER HAT

Stay warm on the slopes or in the city with a boldly striped slouchy hat knit in two layers.

 Inspired by Olympic alpine skier DARON RAHLVES

SIZES
Instructions are given for Child's Medium. Changes for Adult Medium are in parentheses.

KNITTED MEASUREMENTS
• *Brim circumference (unstretched)*
14½ (17)"/37 (43)cm

• *Length*
8½ (10)"/21.5 (25.5)cm

MATERIALS
2 1¾oz/50g balls (each approx 174yd/160m) of Rowan *Pure Wool 4 Ply* (superwash wool) in #436 kiss (A)

1 ball each in #412 snow (B) and #410 indigo (C)

One set (5) size 5 (3.75mm) double-pointed needles (dpns) *or size to obtain gauge*

Stitch markers

GAUGE
34 sts and 34 rnds = 4"/10cm over k1, p1 rib (unstretched) using size 5 (3.75mm) needles.
Take time to check gauge.

❄ DOUBLE-LAYER HAT

K1, P1 RIB
(over an even number of sts)
RND 1 *K1, p1; rep from * to end of rnd.
Rep rnd 1 for k1, p1 rib.

NOTE
Hat is worked in one piece, starting at top of crown of "inner hat" and ending at top of crown of "outer hat."

HAT
TOP OF CROWN (INNER HAT)
With A, cast on 16 sts, distributing evenly over 4 dpns. Join to work in the rnd, being careful not to twist sts, place marker (pm) for beg of rnd. Working in k1, p1 rib throughout, shape top of crown for inner hat as foll:
RND 1 [K1, p1, k1, p1, pm] 3 times, k1, p1, k1, p1.
RND 2 *K1, M1, work in rib to 1 st before marker, M1, sl marker; rep from * to end of rnd—24 sts.
Without placing additional markers, rep rnd 2 another 7 times, then rnds 1 and 2 another 6 (8) times, incorporating new sts into k1, p1 rib—128 (144) sts.
Work even in k1, p1 rib for a further 78 (90) rnds. Break A and join B.
NEXT RND With B, knit.
Work even in k1, p1 rib for a further 26 (30) rnds. Break B and join C.
NEXT RND With C, knit.

CROWN SHAPING (OUTER HAT)
RND 1 Work in rib.
RND 2 *K1, k2tog, work in rib to 2 sts before marker, ssk, sl marker; rep from * 3 times more.

RND 3 Work in rib.
RND 4 *K1, p2tog, work in rib to 2 sts before marker, p2tog, sl marker; rep from * 3 times more—112 (128) sts.
Rep last 4 rnds 2 (3) times more—80 sts.
NEXT RND *K1, k2tog, work in rib to 2 sts before marker, ssk, sl marker; rep from * 3 times more—72 sts.
NEXT RND *K1, p2tog, work in rib to 2 sts before marker, p2tog, sl marker; rep from * 3 times more—64 sts.
Rep last 2 rnds 3 times more—16 sts.
Break yarn, leaving a long tail. Thread tail through rem sts and pull tightly to secure.

FINISHING
Using cast-on tail, gather cast-on sts and close top of inner hat. Fold inner hat to inside of outer hat to create a reversible, double-layered hat.❄

DARON RAHLVES
Daron's red, white, and blue slouchy hat is just his style—American, relaxed, and very, very cool. It says, "Go ahead: try to beat me. I dare ya!"

If it's fast, dangerous, and fun, four-time Olympian Daron Rahlves probably does it and does it well. The 2001 World Super G Champion is the only American with his name painted on a gondola in Kitzbuhel, Austria, an honor reserved for winners of the legendary Hahnenkamm downhill. Before his thirteen-year stint on the U.S. Ski Team, the California boy was a world champion jet skier. After retiring from ski racing, Daron merely shifted gears, competing in ski cross on the 48 Straight Tour, in the X Games, and in the 2010 Vancouver Olympics. In his drive to push the boundaries of the sport, he started the big-mountain Banzai Tour, which hits Tahoe's biggest terrain. Based in Truckee, California, Daron is a local hero in Tahoe and Sugar Bowl's skiing ambassador. He and his wife, Michelle, are raising twins Dreyson and Miley, and occasionally escaping to surf in Encinitas.

DESIGNED BY STEPHANNIE TALLENT

STRIPED FLIP-TOP MITTENS

Brightly colored stripes add a sporty and fun vibe to a pair of wear-everywhere convertible mittens.

Inspired by X Games freestyle skier MICHELLE PARKER

SIZE
Woman's Medium

KNITTED MEASUREMENTS
• *Hand circumference*
  8"/20.5cm

• *Length from cuff to middle fingertip*
  9½"/24cm

MATERIALS
1 7oz/198g skein (each approx 370yd/338m) of Red Heart *With Love* (acrylic) each in #1303 aran (A), #1814 true blue (B), and #1601 lettuce (C)

One set (5) each sizes 4 and 7 (3.5 and 4.5mm) double-pointed needles (dpns) *or size to obtain gauge*

Stitch markers, including removable markers

Small amount of scrap yarn

GAUGE
18 sts and 28 rows = 4"/10cm over St st using size 7 (4.5mm) needles. *Take time to check gauge.*

STITCH GLOSSARY
M1R Insert LH needle from back to front under the strand between last st worked and next st on LH needle.

K into the front loop to twist the st.
M1L Insert LH needle from front to back under the strand between last st worked and next st on LH needle. K into the back loop to twist the st.

K2, P1 RIB
(multiple of 3 sts)
RND 1 *K2, p1; rep from * to end of rnd.
Rep rnd 1 for k2, p1 rib.

LEFT MITTEN
CUFF
With smaller dpns and A, cast on 36 sts and divide evenly over 4 needles. Join to work in the rnd, being careful not to twist sts, and place marker (pm) for beg of rnd. Work 3 rnds in k2, p1 rib.
RND 4 With B, knit.
RND 5 With B, *k2, p1; rep from * to end of rnd.
RND 6 With A, knit.
RND 7 With A, *k2, p1; rep from * to end of rnd.
RND 8 With C, knit.
RNDS 9 AND 10 With C, *k2, p1; rep from * to end of rnd.
RND 11 With A, knit.
RND 12 With A, *k2, p1; rep from * to end of rnd.
RND 13 With B, knit.
RND 14 With B, *k2, p1; rep from * to end of rnd.
RND 15 With A, knit.
RND 16 With A, *k2, p1; rep from * to end of rnd.
Change to larger dpns.

RND 17 K15, pm, k2, pm, k19.

THUMB GUSSET
NEXT RND K15, slip marker (sm), M1R, k2, M1L, sm, k19.
Work 2 rnds even in St st.
Rep last 3 rnds until there are 16 sts between markers in thumb gusset.
NEXT RND K15, place next 16 sts on scrap yarn, cast on 2 sts, k19—36 sts. Knit 5 rnds, marking 17th st with a removable marker.

TOP EDGE
Change to smaller dpns and work 6 rnds in k2, p1 rib. Bind off in rib.

MITTEN FLAP
With larger dpns and A, beg with the st above the marked st,
pick up 20 sts (do not knit), cast on 17 sts and join to work in the rnd.
RND 1 Sl 1, k18, ssk, k15, ssk, pm for beg of rnd—35 sts.
RNDS 2–9 K20, [p1, k2] 5 times.
RND 10 K18, pm for side, k8, M1, k9—36 sts.
RND 11 Knit.
RNDS 12–13 With B, knit.
RNDS 14–15 With A, knit.
RNDS 16–18 With C, knit.
RNDS 19–20 With A, knit.

TOP SHAPING
RND 21 With B, [ssk, knit to 2 sts before marker, k2tog] twice—32 sts.
RND 22 With B, knit.
RND 23 With A, [ssk, knit to 2 sts before marker, k2tog] twice—28 sts.

❄ STRIPED FLIP-TOP MITTENS

RND 24 With A, knit.
Rep last 2 rnds 3 times more—16 sts. Graft sts together using Kitchener st.

RIGHT MITTEN
CUFF
With smaller dpns and A, cast on 36 sts and divide evenly over 4 needles. Join to work in the rnd, being careful not to twist sts, and pm for beg of rnd. Work 3 rnds in k2, p1 rib.
RND 4 With B, knit.
RND 5 With B, *k2, p1; rep from * to end of rnd.
RND 6 With A, knit.
RND 7 With A, *k2, p1; rep from * to end of rnd.
RND 8 With C, knit.
RNDS 9–10 With C, *k2, p1; rep from * to end of rnd.
RND 11 With A, knit.
RND 12 With A, *k2, p1; rep from * to end of rnd.
RND 13 With B, knit.
RND 14 With B, *k2, p1; rep from * to end of rnd.
RND 15 With A, knit.
RND 16 With A, *k2, p1; rep from * to end of rnd.
Change to larger dpns.
RND 17 K19, pm, k2, pm, k15.

THUMB GUSSET
NEXT RND K19, sm, M1R, k2, M1L, sm, k15.
Work 2 rnds even in St st. Rep last 3 rnds until there are 16 sts in gusset.
NEXT RND K19, place next 16 sts on scrap yarn, cast on 2 sts, k15—36 sts. Knit 5 rnds, marking last st with a removable marker.

TOP EDGE
Change to smaller dpns and work 6 rnds in k2, p1 rib. Bind off in rib.

MITTEN FLAP
With larger dpns and A, beg with the st above marked st, pick up 20 sts (do not knit), cast on 17 sts, join to work in the rnd.
RND 1 Sl 1, k18, ssk, k15, ssk, pm for beg of rnd—35 sts.
RNDS 2–9 K20, [p1, k2] 5 times.
RND 10 K18, pm for side, k8, M1, k9—36 sts.
RND 11 Knit.
RNDS 12–13 With B, knit.
RNDS 14–15 With A, knit.
RNDS 16–18 With C, knit.
RNDS 19–20 With A, knit.

TOP SHAPING
RND 21 With B, [ssk, knit to 2 sts before marker, k2tog] twice—32 sts.
RND 22 With B, knit.
RND 23 With A, [ssk, knit to 2 sts before marker, k2tog] twice—28 sts.
RND 24 With A, knit.
Rep last 2 rnds 3 times more—16 sts. Graft sts together using Kitchener st.

THUMBS
Place 16 held thumb sts on larger dpns. Using A, k16, pick up and k 2 sts at base of thumb—18 sts.
RND 1 K1, k2tog, k to last 2 sts, k2tog—16 sts.
RND 2 K2tog, k to end—15 sts.
Work in k2, p1 rib for 4 rnds. Bind off in pattern. ❄

MICHELE PARKER
Michele is totally into fingerless gloves and finds these, with lots of color and a foldover mitten top, "so rad!"

Professional skier and slopestyle champ Michelle Parker never trains. Sure, she skis as much as humanly possible and works on getting better at her sport every day. But, she says, "I never use the word 'training' when it comes to skiing." What does Michelle like to do on skis? "My ultimate goal is to put together a super well-rounded part in a ski movie, with big mountain lines, backcountry jumps, park jumps, and rails." The Squaw Valley kid was on snow at age two, racing by age six, and competing professionally as a freestyle skier at fifteen. She's a regular on both the competitive freeskiing circuit and the big screen, traveling the world in search of big powdery lines. Michele won Best Female Performance at the Powder Video Awards for her segment in *Superheroes of Stoke*. "Filming is where I get the most out of my skiing," she says. When not skiing, Michele likes to hike, mountain bike, explore, camp, and be with family and friends.

DESIGNED BY EDIE ECKMAN

VARIEGATED HAT

Subtle color changes in the wool-blend yarn and a poufy pompom lend pizzazz to an easy-to-knit ribbed hat.

 Inspired by X Games champion freestyle skier DAVID WISE

SIZE
Adult Medium

KNITTED MEASUREMENTS
• *Brim circumference* 20"/51cm

• *Length* 10"/25.5cm

MATERIALS
2 3½oz/100g skeins (each approx 151yd/138m) of Red Heart *Boutique Treasure* (acrylic/wool) in #1901 mosaic OR #1907 portrait

Size 10½ (6.5mm) circular needle, 16"/40cm long, *or size to obtain gauge*

One set (5) size 10½ (6.5mm) double-pointed needles (dpns)

Stitch marker

Pompom maker (optional)

GAUGE
17 sts and 22 rnds = 4"/10cm over St st using size 10.5 (6.5mm) needles. *Take time to check gauge.*

STITCH GLOSSARY
KFB Knit into the front and back of next st—1 st increased.

K1, P1 RIB
(over an even number of sts)
RND 1 *K1, p1; rep from * to end.
Rep rnd 1 for k1, p1 rib.

NOTE
Change to dpns when there are too few sts to fit comfortably on circular needle.

HAT
With circular needle, cast on 80 sts. Join to work in the rnd, being careful not to twist sts, and place marker (pm) for beg of rnd. Work in k1, p1 rib for 3"/7.5cm.
NEXT (INC) RND *K9, kfb; rep from * to end of rnd—88 sts. Cont in St st (knit every rnd) until hat measures 7"/18cm from beg.

❋ VARIEGATED HAT

DAVID WISE
David's hat design is based on one he crocheted for his wife, Lexi. How cute is that? Come on, men, get crafty!

CROWN SHAPING

RND 1 *K9, k2tog; rep from * to end of rnd—80 sts.

**RND 2 AND ALL
EVEN-NUMBERED RNDS** Knit.

RND 3 *K8, ssk; rep from * to end of rnd—72 sts.

RND 5 *K7, k2tog; rep from * to end of rnd—64 sts.

RND 7 *K6, ssk; rep from * to end of rnd—56 sts.

RND 9 *K5, k2tog; rep from * to end of rnd—48 sts.

RND 11 *K4, ssk; rep from * to end of rnd—40 sts.

RND 13 *K3, k2tog; rep from * to end of rnd—32 sts.

RND 15 *K2, ssk; rep from * to end of rnd—24 sts.

RND 17 *K1, k2tog; rep from * to end of rnd—16 sts.

RND 18 *K2tog; rep from * to end of rnd—8 sts.
Break yarn, leaving a long tail.
Thread tail through rem sts and pull tightly to secure.

FINISHING
POMPOM
Make a pompom 3–4"/7.5–10cm in diameter. Sew to top of hat.
Block lightly to measurements. ❋

David Wise, the Reno, Nevada, native who scored gold in X Games superpipe for two consecutive years, was also the first daddy to win superpipe gold. You can often see his young family—wife Lexi and their daughter, Nayeli—cheering him on in the crowd at competitions. Skiing is in the Wise family's blood: David's dad raced in college, and David himself was a ski racer at Mount Rose in Tahoe before the parks and pipes lured him toward the freestyle team at age eleven. Once he combined his passion for skiing with his love of being airborne, there was no turning back. After a superpipe win at the 2009 World Skiing Invitational, David made skiing history by being the first person ever to perform a Double Cork 1260 in the halfpipe. Not surprisingly, David is an inaugural member of the U.S. Freeskiing Halfpipe Team.

RUFFLE SCARF

A merino-alpaca blend that's lightweight but warm gives this scarf an airy feel, accentuated by a bell ruffle.

 Inspired by Olympic champion mogul skier **HANNAH KEARNEY**

KNITTED MEASUREMENTS

- *Width*
  Approx 9"/23cm

- *Length*
  Approx 53"/134.5cm

MATERIALS

4 1¾oz/50g balls (each approx 120yd/110m) of Rowan *Lima* (merino/alpaca/nylon) in #882 Chile (**4**)

One pair size 7 (4.5mm) needles
or size to obtain gauge

GAUGE

20 sts and 27 rows = 4"/10cm over garter stitch rib using size 7 (4.5mm) needles.
Take time to check gauge.

KNITTED CAST-ON

Make a slip knot on LH needle. *Insert RH needle knitwise into st on LH needle. Wrap yarn around RH needle as if to knit. Draw yarn through 1st st to make a new st, but do not drop st from LH needle. Slip new st to LH needle. Rep from * until required number of sts is cast on.

✳RUFFLE SCARF

GARTER STITCH RIB

(multiple of 4 sts plus 3)
ROW 1 (RS) P3, [k1, p3] to end.
ROW 2 Purl.
Rep rows 1 and 2 for garter st rib.

SCARF

Using knitted cast-on,
cast on 135 sts.
Knit 2 rows.

BEG FIRST RUFFLE

NEXT ROW (RS) P3, [k9, p3]
11 times.
NEXT ROW Purl.
Rep last 2 rows 4 times more.
NEXT (DEC) ROW (RS) P3, [ssk, k5,
k2tog, p3] 11 times—113 sts.
NEXT ROW Purl.
NEXT (DEC) ROW P3, [ssk, k3,
k2tog, p3] 11 times—91 sts.
NEXT ROW Purl.
NEXT (DEC) ROW P3, [ssk, k1,
k2tog, p3] 11 times—69 sts.
NEXT ROW Purl.
NEXT (DEC) ROW P3, [S2KP, p3] 11
times—47 sts.
NEXT ROW Purl.

BEG GARTER ST RIB

NEXT ROW (RS) Work row 1 of
garter st rib.
Work even in garter st rib until piece
measures approx 50½"/128cm from
beg, end with a WS row.

BEG SECOND RUFFLE

NEXT (INC) ROW (RS) P3, [M1, k1,
M1, p3] 11 times—69 sts.
NEXT ROW Purl.
NEXT (INC) ROW P3, [M1, k3, M1,
p3] 11 times—91 sts.
NEXT ROW Purl.
NEXT (INC) ROW P3, [M1, k5, M1,
p3] 11 times—113 sts.
NEXT ROW Purl.
NEXT (INC) ROW P3, [M1, k7, M1,
p3] 11 times—135 sts.
NEXT ROW Purl.
NEXT ROW P3, [k9, p3] 11 times.
Rep last 2 rows 4 times more.
Knit 2 rows. Bind off loosely knitwise.

FINISHING

Block lightly to measurements. ✳

HANNAH KEARNEY
Hannah's scarf is based
on one she knit for her
friend as a birthday present
while training in Chile.

Hannah Kearney is a master
at balancing acts, even
when she isn't speeding down
a mogul field. Born in Hanover,
New Hampshire, Kearney was on
skis at age two and started in the
Ford Sayre after-school freestyle
program at age seven. She
honed her skills with the
Waterville Valley Black and Blue
Trail Smashers and, in high
school, became World Junior
Champion in freestyle skiing, in
addition to leading her high
school team to state soccer and
track championships. She
focused on World Cup moguls
full-time in 2004, won her first
world title in 2005, and competed
in her first Olympics in 2006. In
2010 the "half Canadian" (she
has lots of relatives north of the
border) added Olympic gold to
her four national titles and two
overall freestyle World Cup titles.
When not competing, she
attends Dartmouth College and
likes to ride horses, knit (donating
much of her knitting to charity),
play soccer, read, and watch her
brother Denny play hockey.

DESIGNED BY GWEN BORTNER

RIBBED & STRIPED HAT

A basic ribbed hat with a little slouch is modern
and versatile in shades of wintry gray.

 Inspired by X Games champion snowboarder NATE HOLLAND

SIZES
Instructions are written for size
Adult Small/Medium. Changes for
Large are in parentheses.

KNITTED MEASUREMENTS
• *Brim circumference (unstretched)*
13½ (16)"/34 (40.5)cm

• *Length*
7 (8½)"/18 (21.5)cm

MATERIALS
1 3½oz/100g skein (each
approx 126yd/115m) of
Rowan *Cocoon* (merino/mohair)
each in #805 mountain (A),
#803 scree (B), and
#801 polar (C) **⑤**

One set (5) size 9 (5.5mm)
double-pointed needles (dpns)
or size to obtain gauge

Stitch markers

Tapestry needle

GAUGE
26 sts and 24 rnds = 4"/10cm
over k1, p1 rib (unstretched) using
size 9 (5.5mm) needles.
Take time to check gauge.

CABLE CAST-ON
1) Make a slip knot on LH needle.
Insert RH needle knitwise into st
on LH needle. Wrap yarn around RH
needle as if to knit.
2) Draw yarn through 1st st to
make a new st, but do not drop 1st
st from LH needle. Slip new st to LH
needle, to right of 1st st.

3) Insert RH needle between 2 sts on
LH needle. Wrap yarn around RH
needle as if to knit and pull yarn
through to make a new st.
4) Place new st on LH needle, to
right of previous st. Rep steps 3 and
4, always inserting RH needle
between last 2 sts on LH needle.

K1, P1 RIB
(over an even number of sts)
RND 1 *K1, p1, rep from * to end
of rnd.
Rep rnd 1 for k1, p1 rib.

❄RIBBED & STRIPED HAT

HAT

Using cable cast-on and A, cast on 88 (104) sts, dividing evenly over 4 dpns—22 (26) sts on each dpn. Join to work in the rnd, being careful not to twist sts, place marker (pm) for beg of rnd.

With A, work 10 (12) rnds in k1, p1 rib.

NEXT RND With B, knit.

Work 8 (9) rnds in k1, p1 rib.

NEXT RND With A, knit.

Work 8 (9) rnds in k1, p1 rib.

NEXT RND With C, knit.

CROWN SHAPING

RND 1 [K1, k2tog, work to last 2 sts on dpn, ssk] 4 times to end of rnd—20 (24) sts each dpn.

RND 2 AND ALL EVEN-NUMBERED RNDS Work even in rib.

RND 3 [K1, p2tog, work to last 2 sts on dpn, ssp] 4 times to end of rnd—18 (22) sts each dpn.

RND 5 [K1, k2tog, work to last 2 sts on dpn, ssk] 4 times to end of rnd—16 (20) sts each dpn.

RND 7 [K1, p2tog, work to last 2 sts on dpn, ssp] 4 times to end of rnd—14 (18) sts each dpn.

SIZE SMALL/MEDIUM ONLY

RND 8 With A, knit.

RND 9 [K1, k2tog, work to last 2 sts on dpn, ssk] 4 times to end of rnd—12 sts each dpn.

RND 10 Work even in rib.

RND 11 [K1, p2tog, work to last 2 sts on dpn, ssp] 4 times to end of rnd—10 sts each dpn.

RND 12 [K1, k2tog, work to last 2 sts on dpn, ssk] 4 times to end of rnd—8 sts each dpn.

Rep last 2 rnds once more—4 sts each dpn, 16 sts total.

SIZE LARGE ONLY

RND 8 Work even in rib.

RND 9 [K1, k2tog, work to last 2 sts on dpn, ssk] 4 times to end of rnd—16 sts each dpn.

RND 10 With A, knit.

RND 11 [K1, p2tog, work to last 2 sts on dpn, ssp] 4 times to end of rnd—14 sts each dpn.

RND 12 Work even in rib.

RND 13 [K1, k2tog, work to last 2 sts on dpn, ssk] 4 times to end of rnd—12 sts each dpn.

RND 14 [K1, p2tog, work to last 2 sts on dpn, ssp] 4 times to end of rnd—10 sts each dpn.

Rep last 2 rnds once more—6 sts each dpn, 24 sts total.

NEXT RND [K1, k2tog, work to last 2 sts on dpn, ssk] 4 times to end of rnd—4 sts each dpn, 16 sts total.

Break yarn, leaving 10"/25.5cm tail. Thread tail through rem sts, pull tightly to secure.

FINISHING

Block lightly to measurements. ❄

NATE HOLLAND
Nate's design is inspired by a favorite striped hat that's perfect for keeping warm on the slopes and everywhere else.

When boardercross became an Olympic sport in 2006, Nate Holland was there. And he was there four years later in Torino. With six golds in the X Games, Nate's got plenty of medals, but they didn't come from following an ordinary path. The native of Sand Point, Idaho, grew up snowboarding on Schweitzer Mountain. After high school he moved to Mount Hood, where he worked as a parking attendant in exchange for a ski pass. Eventually Nate settled in Tahoe to compete on the snowboard. After his first international competition, he was invited to the X Games and to the first U.S. SBX camp. He won a spot on the team and placed fifth in his first World Cup. The next year he hit the podium, and from there it was "pretty much a snowball effect." When not training or riding, Nate enjoys dirt biking, fly fishing, mountain biking, wakeboarding, and running Action Water Sports on Lake Pend Oreille, Idaho, with his brother, Pat.

KITTEN MITTENS

Warm your hands on wintry days with sweet appliquéd kittens and embroidered snowflakes.

Inspired by X Games medal-winning freestyle skier BRITA SIGOURNEY

SIZE
Woman's Medium

KNITTED MEASUREMENTS
• Hand circumference 9"/23cm

• Length from cuff to middle fingertip 9"/23cm

MATERIALS
1 7oz/198g skein (each approx 370yd/338m) of Red Heart *With Love* (acrylic) each in #1401 pewter (A) and #1303 aran (B) (4)

One 3½oz/100g skein (each approx 307yd/281m) of Red Heart *Luster Sheen* (acrylic) in #0915 cherry red (C) (2)

One set (5) each sizes 7 and 8 (4.5 and 5mm) double-pointed needles (dpns) *or size to obtain gauge*

One pair size 7 (4.5mm) needles

One set (2) size 2 (2.75mm) double-pointed needles

Stitch markers and stitch holder

GAUGE
16 sts and 23 rnds = 4"/10cm over St st using size 8 (5mm) needles. *Take time to check gauge.*

STITCH GLOSSARY
KFB Knit into the front and back of next st—1 st increased.

NOTE
Left and right are determined once the cat appliqué is placed onto the backs of the mittens.

MITTEN (MAKE 2)
With size 7 (4.5mm) dpns and A, cast on 36 sts, distributing evenly over 4 dpns. Join to work in the rnd, being careful not to twist sts, and place marker (pm) for beg of rnd.
RND 1 *With A, k1; with B, k1; rep from * to end of rnd.
RND 2 *With A, k1; with B, p1; rep from * to end of rnd.
Rep rnd 2 until piece measures 2½"/6.5cm from beg. Break B and cont with A only.
NEXT RND With A, knit.
Change to larger dpns and knit a further 4 rnds.

THUMB GUSSET
RND 1 Kfb, k1, kfb, pm, knit to end of rnd.
RND 2 Knit.
RND 3 Kfb, knit to last st before marker, kfb, sl marker, knit to end of rnd.
RND 4 Knit.
Rep last 2 rnds 6 times more—17 sts between markers.

HAND
NEXT RND K1, place next 16 sts on holder or scrap yarn, cast on 2 sts,

knit to end of rnd—36 sts. Work 12 rnds even in St st.

TOP SHAPING
RND 1 *K7, k2tog; rep from * to end of rnd—32 sts.
RNDS 2 AND 3 Knit.
RND 4 *K6, k2tog; rep from * to end of rnd—28 sts.
RNDS 5 AND 6 Knit.
RND 7 *K5, k2tog; rep from * to end of rnd—24 sts.
RNDS 8 AND 9 Knit.
RND 10 *K4, k2tog; rep from * to end of rnd—20 sts.
RNDS 11 AND 12 Knit.
RND 13 *K3, k2tog; rep from * to end of rnd—16 sts.
RNDS 14 AND 15 Knit.
RND 16 *K2, k2tog; rep from * to end of rnd—12 sts.
RND 17 *K1, k2tog; rep from * to end of rnd—8 sts.
Distribute rem 4 sts on 2 needles and graft tog.

THUMB
Arrange 16 sts for thumb over 3 dpns.
RND 1 K16; with 4th dpn, pick up and k 2 sts at base of thumb—18 sts. Distribute sts evenly. Join to work in the rnd and work in St st (k every rnd) for 1½"/4cm.
NEXT RND *K2tog; rep from * to end of rnd—9 sts.

❄️KITTEN MITTENS

NEXT RND [K2tog] 3 times, k3tog—4 sts.
Break yarn, leaving a long tail.
Thread tail through rem sts and pull tightly to secure.

FINISHING
CAT APPLIQUÉ (MAKE 2)
With straight needles and B, cast on 6 sts.
ROW 1 (WS) Sl 1, purl to end of row.
ROW 2 Sl 1, M1, k4, M1, k1—8 sts.
ROWS 3, 5, AND 7 Sl 1, purl to end of row.
ROW 4 Sl 1, M1, k6, M1, k1—10 sts.
ROWS 6 AND 8 Sl 1, k2tog, knit to last 3 sts, k2tog, k1—6 sts.
ROW 9 P1, [p2tog] twice, p1—4 sts.
ROW 10 K1, k2tog, k1—3 sts.
ROWS 11, 13, AND 15 Sl 1, purl to end of row.
ROW 12 Sl 1, M1, k1, M1, k1—5 sts.
ROW 14 Sl 1, M1, k3, M1, k1—7 sts.
ROW 16 K3tog (first ear), break yarn, pull tail through last stitch, rejoin yarn and bind off center st, k3tog (second ear), break yarn, pull tail through last stitch.

I-CORD TAIL
With size 7 (4.5mm) dpn and B, pick up and k 2 sts at base of cat (for left mitten, pick up on right side edge, for right mitten, pick up on left side edge). *Knit one row. Without turning work, sl sts back to beg of row. Pull yarn tightly from end of row. Rep from * until I-cord measures approx 3"/7.5cm. Bind off knitwise.

NECK TIE
With C, cut a 3"/7.5cm length of yarn and tie a bow around the cat's neck. Secure a knot at each end to prevent fraying, and trim. Secure bow in place with 1–2 stitches from front to back, at center knot.
Sew appliqué to mitten, using photo as guide. With B, randomly embroider French knots around appliqué.

FINISHING
CUFF TIE (MAKE 2)
With size 2 (2.75mm) dpns and C, cast on 2 sts. *Knit one row. Without turning work, sl sts back to beg of row. Pull yarn tightly from end of row. Rep from * until I-cord measures approx 18"/46cm or desired length. Bind off knitwise. Thread I-cord through middle of cuff ribbing.

TIE TASSELS
With C, make 2 tassels, each with a finished length of 1½"/4cm. Attach one tassel to each end of cuff tie. Block lightly to measurements. ❄️

BRITA SIGOURNEY
An animal lover, Brita fosters pets from the local shelter whenever she can. "I recently adopted a kitty, Cory. She is such a joy, so obviously when I saw these mittens I had to have them!"

Water or snow—a tough choice for a California girl who excelled at swimming, diving, water polo, and freestyle skiing. But after one year at UC Davis, where she had earned a scholarship to compete in the pool, Brita Sigourney chose snow. Winning the World Junior Championships in New Zealand that summer and making the U.S. Ski Team certainly helped. Growing up in the beach town of Carmel, Brita spent virtually every winter weekend making the five-hour trek to Alpine Meadows in Tahoe, eventually competing in moguls, big air, slope style, and halfpipe events. Since 2010, she has focused exclusively on halfpipe, winning X Games silver and bronze and becoming the first woman to land a 1080-degree spin in competition. When she's not training or competing, she's hitting the books, working toward her college degree.

NORDIC HAT

A traditional snowflake Fair Isle hat goes modern with
a little slouch and a fun multicolored pompom.

 Inspired by Olympic alpine skier TIGER SHAW

SIZE
Adult Medium

KNITTED MEASUREMENTS
• *Brim circumference
(stretched)* 19"/48cm

• *Length*
10½"/26.5cm

MATERIALS
2 1¾oz/50g balls (each approx
120yd/110m) of Rowan *Lima*
(merino/alpaca/nylon) in #891
La Paz (MC)

One ball in #890 Bolivia (CC)

One pair each sizes 7 and 8
(4.5 and 5mm) needles *or size to
obtain gauge*

Pompom maker (optional)

GAUGE
23 sts and 28 rnds = 4"/10cm
over Fair Isle pat using size 8
(5mm) needles.
Take time to check gauge.

K2, P2 RIB
(multiple of 4 sts plus 2)
ROW 1 (RS) *K2, p2; rep from * to
last 2 sts, k2.
ROW 2 *P2, k2; rep from * to last
2 sts, p2.
Rep rows 1 and 2 for k2, p2 rib.

NOTE
Chart is worked back and forth in
rows of St st (k on RS, p on WS)
throughout.

HAT
With smaller needles and CC,
cast on 114 sts. Knit 1 row.
Break CC and join MC. Work in k2,
p2 rib until piece measures 3½"/9cm
from beg, end with a RS row.
NEXT ROW Purl, dec 1 st at center
of row—113 sts.
Change to larger needles.

❋ NORDIC HAT

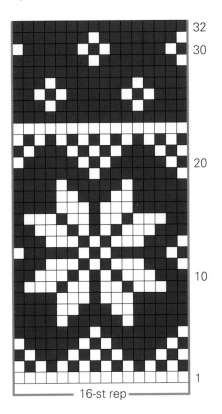

32
30

20

10

1

— 16-st rep —

COLOR KEY

■ La Paz (MC)

□ Bolivia (CC)

BEG CHART

ROW 1 (RS) K1, work row 1 of 16-st rep of chart 7 times.

ROW 2 Work row 2 of 16-st rep of chart 7 times, p1.

Cont in pat as established to end of chart, end with a WS row. Break CC and cont with MC only.

CROWN SHAPING

ROW 1 K1, *k8, k2tog; rep from * to last 2 sts, k2—102 sts.

Work 3 rows even in St st.

ROW 5 K1, *k7, k2tog; rep from * to last 2 sts, k2—91 sts.

ROWS 6 AND 8 Purl.

ROW 7 K1, *k6, k2tog; rep from * to last 2 sts, k2—80 sts.

ROW 9 K1, *k5, k2tog; rep from * to last 2 sts, k2—69 sts.

ROW 10 P2, *p2tog, p4; rep from * to last st, p1—58 sts.

ROW 11 K1, *k3, k2tog; rep from * to last 2 sts, k2—47 sts.

ROW 12 P2, *p2tog, p2; rep from * to last st, p1—36 sts.

ROW 13 *K2tog; rep from * to end of row—18 sts.

Break yarn, leaving a long tail. Thread tail through rem sts and fasten off.

FINISHING

Sew center back seam, reversing last 2"/5cm of brim for turnback.

POMPOM

Using one strand of each yarn held together, make a pompom 4"/10cm in diameter. Sew to top of hat.❋

TIGER SHAW

Tiger's hat reminds him of his college days and the famous Dartmouth snowflake.

Two-time Olympian Tiger Shaw might possibly bleed green. A native of Stowe, Vermont, Tiger excelled on the slopes at an early age. He became a standout technical skier for the U.S. Ski Team in the eighties, earning his first of four national GS titles in 1983, the same year he won the NCAA GS title. He went on to compete in the 1984 and 1988 Olympics and graduated from Dartmouth College in 1985 with an engineering degree. When Tiger wasn't studying or on the road, he was designing the house he built in his "spare time." Tiger now works for the medical evacuation service Global Rescue and, since his retirement from skiing, has been on the U.S. Ski Team Board of Trustees. He and his wife, Kristin, raised three ski racers, with Tiger coaching them in the Ford Sayre Program at the Dartmouth Skiway. Their oldest son, Gunnar, now attends (where else?) Dartmouth.

GAITER & MITTENS

A bright graphic motif livens up this super-warm set that includes a tall neck gaiter and mittens.

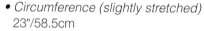 Inspired by X Games medal-winning freestyle skier DEVIN LOGAN

SIZE
Adult Medium

KNITTED MEASUREMENTS
NECK GAITER
- *Circumference (slightly stretched)* 23"/58.5cm
- *Height* 12"/30.5cm

MITTENS
- *Hand circumference* 8"/20.5cm
- *Length to middle fingertip* 10"/25.5cm

MATERIALS
1 7oz/198g skein (each approx 370yd/338m) of Red Heart *With Love* (acrylic) each in #1101 eggshell (MC) and #1803 blue Hawaii (CC)

One pair size 8 (5mm) needles *or size to obtain gauge*

One set (5) size 8 (5mm) double-pointed needles (dpns)

Stitch holder or scrap yarn

GAUGE
16 sts and 21 rows = 4"/10cm over St st using size 8 (5mm) needles. *Take time to check gauge.*

K1, P1 RIB
(over an odd number of sts)
ROW 1 (RS) *K1, p1; rep from * to last st, k1.
ROW 2 P1, *k1, p1; rep from * to end.
Rep rows 1 and 2 for k1, p1 rib.

NOTES
1) Mittens and neck gaiter are knit flat, working back and forth in rows.
2) "X" motif is worked in duplicate stitch after pieces are completed.

GAITER
With straight needles and MC, cast on 93 sts.
Work in k1, p1 rib until piece measures 10"/25.5cm, end with a WS row.
Starting with a knit (RS) row, work 8 rows in St st (k on RS, p on WS), ending with a WS row.
Work a further 4 rows in k1, p1 rib.
Break MC and join CC. Bind off all sts knitwise.
Following chart, work duplicate st over band of St st using CC.

FINISHING
Sew center back seam. Block lightly to measurements.

MITTENS (MAKE 2)
With straight needles and CC, cast on 33 sts.
ROW 1 (WS) Purl 1 row. Break CC and join MC.
ROW 2 With MC, knit.
Starting with row 2, work in k1, p1 rib until piece measures 3"/7.5cm from beg, ending with a WS row.
Starting with a knit (RS) row, work 2½"/6.5cm in St st, ending with a WS row.

THUMB GUSSET
NEXT ROW (RS) K19, place last 5 sts worked onto holder or scrap yarn for thumb, knit to end—28 sts.
NEXT ROW P14, cast on 5 sts, p14—33 sts.
Cont even in St st until piece measures 9"/23cm, end with a WS row.

TOP SHAPING
ROW 1 (RS) *K2, k2tog; rep from * to last st, k1—25 sts.
ROW 2 AND ALL WS ROWS Purl.
ROW 3 *K1, k2tog; rep from * to last st, k1—17 sts.
ROW 5 *K2tog; rep from * to last st, k1—9 sts.
Break yarn, leaving a long tail.
Thread tail through rem sts and pull tightly to secure.

✳ GAITER & MITTENS

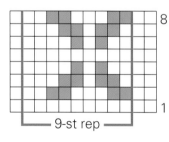

── 9-st rep ──

COLOR KEY

☐ Eggshell (MC)

■ Blue Hawaii (CC)

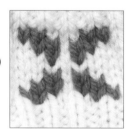

DEVIN LOGAN
Devin's matching gaiter and mittens have a hip, casual look that perfectly complements her style.

Little sibs get off to a fast start. Just ask Vermonter Devin Logan, who used to follow her older brothers to their competitions every winter weekend. When she was six, her mom told her that she might as well compete herself. She wanted to be an alpine racer, but her brothers—pro skiers Sean and Chris—wouldn't allow it. Taking their advice turned out okay: at fifteen she was on the podium at the U.S. Championships, finishing second in halfpipe. Two years later, in her first full season, she made her X Games debut and won a halfpipe bronze. She finished the season with the U.S. halfpipe skiing title and the overall AFP crown. One of few women to excel at both superpipe and slopestyle, she was named to the inaugural U.S. Freeskiing Team for both. When not skiing, Devin stays active with soccer, outdoor adventures, logging hours on the trampoline… and showing her brothers a thing or two.

THUMB

RND 1 With dpns and MC, k5 from stitch holder, pick up and k 7 sts along cast-on edge of thumb opening, distributing sts evenly over 4 dpns—12 sts. Knit 15 rnds or desired length for thumb.
NEXT RND *K2tog; rep from * to end of rnd—6 sts.
Break yarn, leaving a long tail. Thread tail through rem sts and pull tightly to secure.

FINISHING

Using photo as guide, work chart 3 times in duplicate st along front of each mitten, centering "X" between thumb and seam. Sew side seam. Block lightly to measurements. ✳

DESIGNED BY ALEXANDRA TINSLEY

RIBBED SKI CAP

A folded-under brim in a contrasting color adds extra warmth and extra style to a classic ribbed beanie.

 Inspired by Olympic alpine skier EDIE THYS MORGAN

SIZE
Instructions are written for size Medium.

KNITTED MEASUREMENTS
• *Brim circumference (stretched)* 20"/51cm

• *Length 8"/20.5cm*

MATERIALS
1 1¾oz/50g ball (each approx 120yd/110m) of Rowan *Lima* (merino/alpaca/nylon) each in #891 La Paz (MC) and #893 Argentina (CC) (4)

Size 8 (5mm) circular needle, 16"/40cm long, *or size to obtain gauge*

One set (5) size 8 (5mm) double-pointed needles (dpns)

Stitch marker

GAUGE
20 sts and 26 rnds = 4"/10cm over k1, p1 rib, slightly stretched, using size 8 (5mm) needles. *Take time to check gauge.*

K1, P1 RIB
(over an even number of sts)
RND 1 *K1, p1; rep from * to end.
Rep rnd 1 for k1, p1 rib.

NOTES
1) This yarn grows significantly when blocked. Make sure to block your swatch in order to get an accurate gauge.
2) Change to dpns when there are too few sts to fit comfortably on circular needle.

✳RIBBED SKI CAP

EDIE THYS MORGAN

Edie's hat is inspired by her first Squaw Valley Ski Team hat (featured on the cover of her book, *Shut Up and Ski*). "It was red with an American flag on the front, and every single person on our team wore it. I'm not sure I wore any other hat for a few years."

The youngest of four kids in an all ski-racing family, Edie Thys Morgan grew up chasing her siblings all over the mountain at Squaw Valley in California. That may be what made her into a top downhill and super-G skier on the U.S. Ski Team. After retiring from competition, the two-time Olympian (1988, 1992) created the popular column "Racer eX" for *Ski Racing* and *SKI* magazines and became an editor at *SKI*. Now a freelance writer and author, Edie lives in New Hampshire, where she and her husband (ski racer Chan Morgan) coach for the Ford Sayre Ski Club. Their two sons have continued the family tradition of racing around mountains from Squaw Valley to Jackson Hole to the Dartmouth Skiway.

HAT

With circular needle and CC, cast on 88 sts. Join to work in the rnd, being careful not to twist sts, and place marker (pm) for beg of rnd.
Work in k1, p1 rib for 2"/5cm.
Break CC and join MC.
Cont in k1, p1 rib until hat measures 9½"/24cm from beg.

CROWN SHAPING

RND 1 *[K1, p1] 3 times, k2tog; rep from * to end of rnd—77 sts.
RND 2 *[K1, p1] 3 times, k1; rep from * to end of rnd.
RND 3 *[K1, p1] twice, k1, k2tog; rep from * to end of rnd—66 sts.
RND 4 *[K1, p1] twice, k2; rep from * to end of rnd.
RND 5 *[K1, p1] twice, k2tog; rep from * to end of rnd—55 sts.
RND 6 *K1, p1, k1, k2tog; rep from * to end of rnd—44 sts.
RND 7 *K1, p1, k2tog; rep from * to end of rnd—33 sts.
RND 8 *K1, k2tog; rep from * to end of rnd—22 sts.
RND 9 *K2tog; rep from * to end of rnd—11 sts.
Break yarn, leaving a long tail. Thread tail through rem sts and pull tightly to secure.

FINISHING

Fold 2"/5cm CC brim to inside and sew loosely in place. Block lightly to measurements.❄

GRANDPA VEST

A rustic vest in a tweedy blend of warm fibers is the ultimate cozy and easy-to-wear layer.

 Inspired by X Games snowboarding medalist JAYSON HALE

SIZES

Instructions are written for size unisex X-Small. Changes for Small, Medium, Large, X-Large, and XX-Large are in parentheses. (Shown in size Medium.)

KNITTED MEASUREMENTS

• Chest
34 (38, 42, 46, 50, 54)"/86.5 (96.5, 106.5, 117, 127, 137)cm

• Length
24½ (25½, 26½, 27½, 28½, 29½)"/62 (65, 67.5, 70, 72.5, 75)cm

MATERIALS

4 (5, 5, 6, 7, 8) 1¾oz/50g balls (each approx 191yd/175m) of Rowan *Felted Tweed DK* (merino/alpaca/viscose) in #178 seasalter (MC) ④

1 ball in #154 ginger (CC)

One pair size 4 (3.5mm) needles *or size to obtain gauge*

Stitch markers and stitch holders

Eight buttons, ½"/13mm diameter

GAUGE

20 sts and 28 rows = 4"/10cm over St st using size 4 (3.5mm) needles. *Take time to check gauge.*

K1, P1 RIB

(over an odd number of sts)
ROW 1 (RS) *K1, p1; rep from * to last st, k1.
ROW 2 P1, *k1, p1; rep from * to end.
Rep rows 1 and 2 for k1, p1 rib.

K1, P1 RIB

(over an even number of sts)
ROW 1 (RS) *K1, p1; rep from * to end.
ROW 2 *P1, k1; rep from * to end.
Rep rows 1 and 2 for k1, p1 rib.

STITCH GLOSSARY

RT K2tog but do not drop sts from LH needle, k the first st again, drop both sts from needle.

NOTES

1) Wind small amounts of CC onto yarn bobbins.
2) When working with CC, float MC across back (WS) of work.

BACK

With MC, cast on 81 (91, 101, 111, 121, 131) sts. Starting with row 2 (WS), work in k1, p1 rib for 2½"/6.5cm, end with a RS row.
NEXT (INC) ROW (WS) Work in rib, inc 4 sts evenly across—85 (95, 105, 115, 125, 135) sts.
Beg with a RS row, work in St st until piece measures 15½ (16, 16½, 17, 17½, 18)"/39.5 (40.5, 42, 43, 44.5, 45.5)cm from beg; end with a WS row.

ARMHOLE SHAPING

Bind off 3 sts at beg of next 2 (2, 4, 4, 6, 6) rows, 2 sts at beg of next 2 (2, 2, 4, 4, 4) rows—75 (85, 89, 95, 99, 109) sts.
NEXT (DEC) ROW (RS) K1, k2tog, knit to last 3 sts, ssk, k1—73 (83, 87, 93, 97, 107) sts.
Rep dec row every RS row 1 (2, 2, 3, 4, 5) times more—71 (79, 83, 87, 89, 97) sts. Work even until armhole measures 8½ (9, 9½, 10, 10½, 11)"/21.5 (23, 24, 25.5, 26.5, 28)cm, end with a WS row.

NECK AND SHOULDER SHAPING

NEXT ROW (RS) K17 (20, 22, 23, 24, 27), join a 2nd ball of yarn and bind off center 37 (39, 39, 41, 41, 43) sts, knit to end.
Working both sides at once, dec 1 st from neck edge every other row twice, AT THE SAME TIME, bind off from each shoulder edge 5 (6, 7, 7, 7, 8) sts twice, then rem 5 (6, 6, 7, 8, 9) sts.

POCKETS (MAKE 2)

With MC, cast on 17 sts. Beg with a RS row, work in St st until piece measures 3"/7.5cm from beg, end with a WS row. Leave sts on holder.

RIGHT FRONT

With MC, cast on 48 (52, 58, 62, 68, 74) sts. Starting with row 2 (WS), work in k1, p1 rib for 2½"/6.5cm, end with a WS row.

❄ GRANDPA VEST

SET-UP ROW (RS) With MC, k1, [p1, k1] 3 times, k9 (10, 11, 12, 14, 15), M1, k9 (10, 11, 12, 14, 15); with CC, RT; with MC, k2; with CC, RT; with MC, k9 (10, 11, 12, 14, 15), [M1] 0 (1, 0, 1, 0, 1) times, knit to end—49 (54, 59, 64, 69, 76) sts.
ROW 1 (WS) With MC, p17 (20, 23, 26, 27, 32); with CC, p2; with MC, p2; with CC, p2; with MC, p19 (21, 23, 25, 29, 31), [k1, p1] 3 times, k1.
ROW 2 (RS) With MC, k1, [p1, k1] 3 times, k19 (21, 23, 25, 29, 31); with CC, RT; with MC, k2; with CC, RT; with MC, knit to end.
Cont as established until piece measures 5½"/14cm from beg, end with a WS row.
NEXT ROW (RS) Work in pat for 9 (9, 9, 11, 11, 11) sts, place marker (pm), p1, [k1, p1] 7 times, pm, work in pat to end.
NEXT ROW Work in pat to marker, slip marker (sm), [k1, p1] 7 times, k1, sm, work in pat to end.
NEXT ROW Work in pat to marker, sm, k1, [p1, k1] 7 times, sm, work in pat to end.
Rep last 2 rows once more.
NEXT ROW (WS) Work in pat to marker, sm, bind off next 15 sts in rib, sm, work in pat to end.

JOIN POCKET TO RIGHT FRONT
NEXT (JOINING) ROW (RS) Pat to 1 st before 1st marker, sl next st to RH needle, remove marker, place 17 sts from first pocket onto LH needle, sl last st back to LH needle, ssk, knit next 15 sts from first pocket, k2tog, remove 2nd marker and work in pat to end—49 (54, 59, 64, 69, 76) sts.
Cont even in pat until piece measures 15½ (16, 16½, 17, 17½, 18)"/39.5 (40.5, 42, 43, 44.5, 45.5)cm from beg, end with a RS row.

ARMHOLE AND NECK SHAPING
Bind off 3 sts at beg of next 1 (1, 2, 2, 3, 3) WS rows, 2 sts at beg of next 1 (1, 1, 2, 2, 2) WS rows—44 (49, 51, 54, 56, 63) sts.
NEXT (DEC) ROW (RS) Work in pat to last 3 sts, k2tog, k1—43 (48, 50, 53, 55, 62) sts.
Rep dec row every RS row 1 (2, 2, 3, 4, 5) times more, end with a WS row—42 (46, 48, 50, 51, 57) sts.
NEXT (DEC) ROW (RS) Work in pat for 8 sts, ssk, work in pat to end of row—41 (45, 47, 49, 50, 56) sts.
Work 1 row even in pat.
Rep last 2 rows 19 (20, 20, 21, 21, 24) times more—22 (25, 27, 28, 29, 32) sts.
Work even in pat until armhole measures 8½ (9, 9½, 10, 10½, 11)"/21.5 (23, 24, 25.5, 26.5, 28)cm, end with a RS row.

SHOULDER SHAPING
Bind off 5 (6, 7, 7, 7, 8) sts at beg of next 2 WS rows, 5 (6, 6, 7, 8, 9) sts at beg of next WS row—7 sts.

NECKBAND EXTENSION
Cont even in pat on rem 7 sts until extension measures 4 (4¼, 4¼, 4½, 4½, 4¾)"/10 (11, 11, 11.5, 11.5, 12)cm from last bound-off row. Bind off rem 7 sts in pat.
Mark position for 8 buttons along first 7 sts at center front edge, placing the first button ½"/1.5cm from cast-on edge and the last ½"/1.5cm down from start of neck shaping and the rem 6 spaced evenly between.

LEFT FRONT
Work buttonholes opposite markers on right front as foll:
NEXT (BUTTONHOLE) ROW (RS) Work in pat to last 5 sts, yo, p2tog, work in pat to end.

With MC, cast on 48 (52, 58, 62, 68, 74) sts. Starting with row 2 (WS), work in k1, p1 rib for 2½"/6.5cm, end with a WS row.
SET-UP ROW (RS) With MC, k8 (9, 12, 12, 13, 15), [M1] 0 (1, 0, 1, 0, 1) times, k9 (10, 11, 13, 14, 16); with CC, RT; with MC, k2; with CC, RT; with MC, k9 (10, 11, 12, 14, 15), M1, k9 (10, 11, 12, 14, 15), [k1, p1] 3 times, k1—49 (54, 59, 64, 69, 76) sts.
ROW 1 (WS) With MC, p1, [k1, p1] 3 times, p19 (21, 23, 25, 29, 31); with CC, p2; with MC, p2; with CC, p2; with MC, purl to end.
ROW 2 (RS) With MC, k17 (20, 23, 26, 27, 32); with CC, RT; with MC, k2; with CC, RT; with MC, k19 (21, 23, 25, 29, 31), [k1, p1] 3 times, k1.
Cont as established until piece measures 5½"/14cm from beg, end with a WS row.
NEXT ROW (RS) Work in pat for 25 (30, 35, 38, 43, 50) sts, pm, p1, [k1, p1] 7 times, pm, work in pat for 9 (9, 9, 11, 11, 11) sts.
NEXT ROW Work in pat to marker, sm, [k1, p1] 7 times, k1, sm, work in pat to end.
NEXT ROW Work in pat to marker, sm, k1, [p1, k1] 7 times, sm, work in pat to end.
Rep last 2 rows once more.
NEXT ROW (WS) Work in pat to marker, sm, bind off next 15 sts in rib, sm, work in pat to end.

JOIN POCKET TO RIGHT FRONT
NEXT (JOINING) ROW (RS) Work in pat to 1 st before first marker, sl next st to RH needle, remove marker, place 17 sts from second pocket onto LH needle, sl last st back to LH needle, ssk, knit next 15 sts from second pocket, k2tog, remove 2nd marker and work in pat to end—

✳GRANDPA VEST

49 (54, 59, 64, 69, 76) sts.
Cont even in pat until piece
measures 15½ (16, 16½, 17,
17½, 18)"/39.5 (40.5, 42, 43, 44.5,
45.5)cm from beg, end with
a WS row.

ARMHOLE AND NECK SHAPING
Bind off 3 sts at beg of next 1 (1, 2,
2, 3, 3) RS rows, 2 sts at beg of next
1 (1, 1, 2, 2, 2) RS rows—44 (49, 51,
54, 56, 63) sts.
NEXT (DEC) ROW (RS) K1, ssk,
work in pat to end—43 (48, 50, 53,
55, 62) sts.
Rep dec row every RS row 1 (2, 2, 3,
4, 5) times more, end with a WS
row—42 (46, 48, 50, 51, 57) sts.
NEXT (DEC) ROW (RS) Work in pat
to last 8 sts, k2tog, work in pat to
end—41 (45, 47, 49, 50, 56) sts.
Work 1 row even in pat.
Rep last 2 rows 19 (20, 20, 21,
21, 24) times more—22 (25, 27,
28, 29, 32) sts.
Work even in pat until armhole
measures 8½ (9, 9½, 10,
10½,11)"/21.5 (23, 24, 25.5, 26.5,
28)cm, end with a WS row.

SHOULDER SHAPING
Bind off 5 (6, 7, 7, 7, 8) sts at beg of
next 2 RS rows, 5 (6, 6, 7, 8, 9) sts at
beg of next RS row—7 sts.

NECKBAND EXTENSION
Cont even in pat on rem 7 sts until
extension measures 4 (4¼, 4¼, 4½,
4½, 4¾)"/10 (11, 11, 11.5, 11.5,
12)cm from last bound-off row.
Bind off rem 7 sts in pat.

FINISHING
Block pieces to finished
measurements. Sew shoulder
seams. Sew side edges of pocket in
position on WS. Sew bound-off
ends of right and left neckband
extension and sew evenly to back
neck opening.

ARMHOLE EDGING
With RS facing and MC, pick up and
k 93 (99, 103, 111, 119, 125) sts
evenly around armhole opening.
Work in k1, p1 rib for 1"/2.5cm.
Bind off all sts in rib. Sew side and
armhole edging seam.
Sew buttons to right front, opposite
buttonholes.✳

JAYSON HALE
This piece commemorates
one of Jayson's favorite
sweater vests. "It has
been with me for a very
long time, including
traveling on tour with me
for four years."

Jayson Hale fell in love with
snowboarding the hard way—by
breaking his skis on a jump at
age four. Fortunately his cousin
was there, offering him a ride on
a very big snowboard. He
straight-lined it to the bottom and
was hooked, ditching his skis for
good. He started competing at
age six and has been a member
of the U.S. Snowboarding Team
since SBX became an Olympic
sport in 2003. The two-time X
Games medalist was named to
the 2006 Olympic team, but
injuries kept him out of the action
that year and again in 2010. In
the off-season, when not training
at Park City, Utah's USSA Center
of Excellence, Jason spends his
time hunting, fishing, and feeding
a strong environmental ethic. He
spent one summer building trails
for the Sierra Nevada Alliance
near his hometown of Sierraville,
California. No slave to any fashion
but his own, Jayson has been
known to rock a blond mullet.

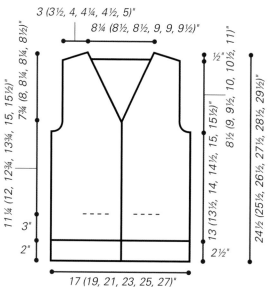

3 (3½, 4, 4¼, 4½, 5)"
8¼ (8½, 8½, 9, 9, 9½)"
7¾ (8, 8¼, 8¼, 8½)"
11¼ (12, 12¾, 13¾, 15, 15½)"
½"
13 (13½, 14, 14½, 15, 15½)"
8½ (9, 9½, 10, 10½, 11)"
24½ (25½, 26½, 27½, 28½, 29½)"
3"
2"
2½"
17 (19, 21, 23, 25, 27)"

SNOWFLAKE TURTLENECK

What could be better for cold weather than a cozy turtleneck with a subtle snowflake stitch pattern on the front?

 Inspired by Olympic champion alpine skier PICABO STREET

SIZE

Instructions are written for women's size X-Small. Changes for Small, Medium, Large, X-Large, and XX-Large are in parentheses. (Shown in size Medium.)

KNITTED MEASUREMENTS

- *Bust*
  34 (38, 42, 46, 50, 54)"/86.5 (96.5, 106.5, 117, 127, 137)cm

- *Length*
  26 (26½, 27, 27½, 28, 28½)"/66 (67.5, 68.5, 70, 71, 72.5)cm

- *Upper arm*
  13½ (14½, 15½, 16½, 17½, 19½)"/34.5 (37, 39.5, 42, 44.5, 49.5)cm

MATERIALS

7 (7, 8, 9, 10, 11) 7oz/198g skeins (each approx 370yd/338m) of Red Heart *With Love* (acrylic) in #1303 aran ④

Size 9 (5.5mm) circular needle, 32"/80cm long, *or size to obtain gauge*

Size 8 (5mm) circular needle, 16"/40cm long

One pair size 9 (5.5mm) needles

Stitch markers and stitch holders

GAUGE

16 sts and 24 rows = 4"/10cm over St st using size 9 (5.5mm) needles. *Take time to check gauge.*

K2, P2 RIB

(multiple of 4 sts)
RND 1 *K2, p2; rep from * to end of rnd.
Rep rnd 1 for k2, p2 rib.

SNOWFLAKE PATTERN

(in the rnd, multiple of 10 sts plus 7)

✳SNOWFLAKE TURTLENECK

RNDS 1, 3, AND 5 K1, *k5, sl 5 wyif; rep from * to last 6 sts, k6.

RNDS 2 AND 4 Knit.

RND 6 K8, *insert RH needle down through 3 loose strands below next st, k these 3 strands tog with next st on needle, k9; rep from *, ending last rep k8.

RNDS 7, 9, AND 11 K1, *sl 5 wyif, k5; rep from * to last 6 sts, sl 5 wyif, k1.

RNDS 8 AND 10 Knit.

RND 12 K3, *insert RH needle down through 3 loose strands below next st, k these 3 strands tog with next st on needle, k9; rep from *, ending last rep k3.

Rep rnds 1–12 for snowflake pat.

SNOWFLAKE PATTERN
(in rows, multiple of 10 sts plus 7)

ROWS 1, 3, AND 5 (RS) K1, *k5, sl 5 wyif; rep from * to last 6 sts, k6.

ROWS 2 AND 4 Purl.

ROW 6 P8, *insert RH needle down through 3 loose strands below next st, p these 3 strands tog with next st on needle, p9; rep from *, ending last rep p8.

ROWS 7, 9, AND 11 K1, *sl 5 wyif, k5; rep from * to last 6 sts, sl 5 wyif, k1.

ROWS 8 AND 10 Purl.

ROW 12 P3, *insert RH needle down through 3 loose strands below next st, p these 3 strands tog with next st on needle, p9; rep from *, ending last rep p3.

Rep rows 1–12 for snowflake pat.

SHORT ROW WRAP & TURN (W&T)
on RS row (on WS row)

1) Wyib (wyif), sl next st purlwise.

2) Move yarn between needles to the front (back).

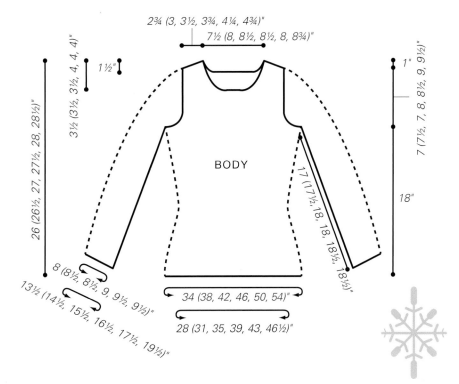

2¾ (3, 3½, 3¾, 4¼, 4¾)"

7½ (8, 8½, 8½, 8, 8¾)"

1½"

3½ (3½, 3½, 4, 4, 4)"

1"

7 (7½, 7, 8, 8½, 9, 9½)"

26 (26½, 27, 27½, 28, 28½)"

BODY

17 (17½, 18, 18, 18½, 18½)"

18"

8 (8½, 8½, 9, 9½, 9½)"

13½ (14½, 15½, 16½, 17½, 19½)"

34 (38, 42, 46, 50, 54)"

28 (31, 35, 39, 43, 46½)"

3) Sl the same st back to LH needle. Turn work. One st is wrapped.

4) When working wrapped st, insert RH needle under wrap and work it tog with corresponding st on needle.

NOTES

1) Body is worked in one piece to armhole.

2) Markers placed on row 3 of body are used for placement of snowflake pattern. Slip markers until snowflake pattern placement.

3) During front armhole decreases, if there are not enough sts to complete snowflake rep, work these rem sts on either side in St st.

4) Sleeves are worked from the top down, working short rows for cap shaping.

BODY

With larger circular needle, cast on 128 (144, 160, 176, 192, 210) sts. Join to work in the rnd, being careful not to twist sts, and place marker (pm) for beg of rnd.

RND 1 K64 (72, 80, 88, 96, 105), pm for side, knit to end.

RNDS 2 AND 4 Purl.

RND 3 K8 (7, 6, 5, 9, 9), pm, k47 (57, 67, 77, 77, 87), pm, knit to end of rnd.

RNDS 5–11 Knit.

NEXT (DEC) RND K2, k2tog, knit to 4 sts before side marker, ssk, k2, slip marker (sm), k2, k2tog, knit to last 4 sts, ssk, k2—124 (140, 156, 172, 188, 206) sts.

Cont in St st, working dec rnd every 12th (10th, 10th, 10th, 10th, 8th) rnd 3 (4, 4, 4, 4, 5) times more—112 (124, 140, 156, 172, 186) sts. Work even in rnds until piece measures 10"/25.5cm from beg.

NEXT (INC) RND K2, M1, knit to 2 sts before side marker, M1, k2, sm, k2, M1, knit to last 2 sts, M1, k2—116 (128, 144, 160, 176, 190) sts. Rep inc rnd every 6th (5th, 5th, 5th,

❄SNOWFLAKE TURTLENECK

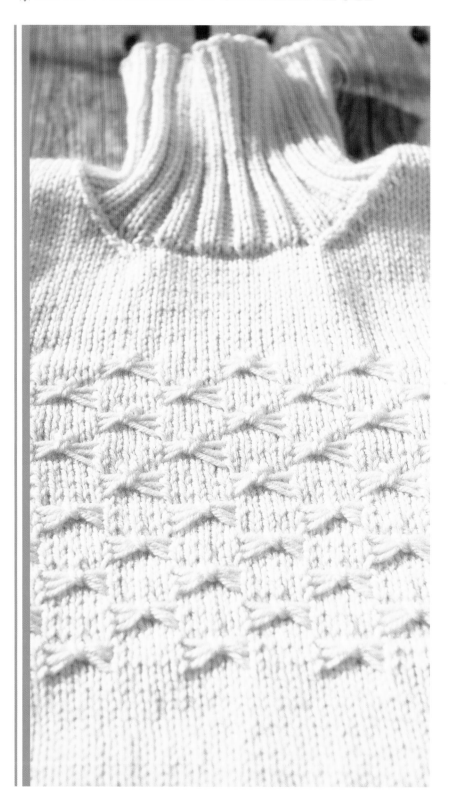

5th, 4th) row 5 (6, 6, 6, 6, 7) times more, AT THE SAME TIME, when work measures 12½"/32cm, work snowflake pat between snowflake markers—136 (152, 168, 184, 200, 218) sts.
Cont even in pat until piece measures 18"/45.5cm.
NEXT RND Work in pat to last 4 (5, 6, 7, 8, 9) sts.

DIVIDE FOR FRONT AND BACK
NEXT RND Bind off last 4 (5, 6, 7, 8, 9) sts of previous rnd, bind off next 4 (5, 6, 7, 8, 9) sts, work in pat for 60 (66, 72, 78, 84, 91) sts and place these sts on holder for front, bind off next 8 (10, 12, 14, 16, 18) sts, knit rem 60 (66, 72, 78, 84, 91) sts for back.

BACK
ARMHOLE SHAPING
Working in St st (k on RS, p on WS) on these 60 (66, 72, 78, 84, 91) sts only, dec 1 st at each end of 3rd and then every following 4th (4th, 4th, 4th, 4th, 2nd) row 3 (4, 5, 6, 7, 8) times—52 (56, 60, 64, 68, 73) sts.
Work even in St st until armhole measures 6½ (7, 7½, 8, 8½, 9)"/15 (18, 20.5, 23, 23, 25.5)cm, end with a WS row.

NECK AND SHOULDER SHAPING
NEXT ROW (RS) K14 (15, 17, 18, 20, 22), join a 2nd ball of yarn and bind off center 24 (26, 26, 28, 28, 29) sts, knit to end.
Working both sides at same time, dec 1 st at each neck edge every row 3 times—11 (12, 14, 15, 17, 19) sts rem each side for shoulder.
Bind off from each shoulder edge 3 (4, 4, 5, 5, 7) sts once, 4 (4, 5, 5, 6, 6) sts twice.

FRONT

Place 60 (66, 72, 78, 84, 91) sts from front holder onto needle, ready for a WS row.

Keeping continuity of pat, dec 1 st at each end of 3rd and then every following 4th (4th, 4th, 4th, 4th, 2nd) row 3 (4, 5, 6, 7, 8) times—52 (56, 60, 64, 68, 73) sts.

Work even in St st until armhole measures 4½ (5, 5½, 5½, 6, 6½)"/11.5 (12.5, 14, 14, 15, 16.5)cm, end with a WS row.

NECK AND SHOULDER SHAPING

NEXT ROW (RS) K18 (20, 22, 24, 25, 27), join a 2nd ball of yarn and bind off center 16 (16, 16, 16, 18, 19) sts, knit to end of row.

Working both sides at same time, dec 1 st at each neck edge every row 7 (8, 8, 9, 8, 8) times—11 (12, 14, 15, 17, 19) sts rem each side for shoulder. Work even until piece measures same as back to shoulder. Bind off from each shoulder edge 3 (4, 4, 5, 5, 7) sts once, 4 (4, 5, 5, 6, 6) sts twice.

SLEEVES

Sew shoulder seams.

With larger circular needle and RS facing, begin at center of underarm and pick up and k 64 (60, 76, 82, 88, 98) sts evenly around armhole opening. Pm for beg of rnd.

RND 1 Knit.

SHAPE SLEEVE CAP

ROW 2 (RS) K38 (36, 44, 47, 50, 55), w&t.
ROW 3 P12, w&t.
ROW 4 K13, w&t.

Cont as established, working 1 st more every row until 28 (28, 28, 28, 28, 32) sts have been worked.

NEXT ROW (RS) K1, k2tog, k26 (26, 26, 26, 26, 30), w&t.

NEXT ROW P1, p2tog, p26 (26, 26, 26, 26, 30), w&t.

Rep last 2 rows 4 (5, 6, 7, 8, 9) times more.

NEXT ROW (RS) K29 (29, 29, 29, 29, 33), w&t.

NEXT ROW P30 (30, 30, 30, 30, 34), w&t.

Cont as est, working 1 st more every row until 4 (5, 6, 7, 8, 9) sts rem unworked at each end of needle—54 (58, 62, 66, 70, 78) sts total.

NEXT ROW (RS) Knit.
NEXT ROW Purl.

Change to straight needles. Working back and forth in rows, cont in St st, dec 1 st at each end of 8th (6th, 6th, 6th, 6th, 4th) row 11 (2, 10, 13, 16, 12) times, then every 8th (8th, 8th, 8th, 6th, 6th) row 0 (10, 4, 2, 0, 8) times—32 (34, 34, 36, 38, 38) sts.

Work even until sleeve measures 16¾ (16¾, 17¼, 17¼, 17¾, 17¾)"/42.5 (42.5, 44, 44, 45, 45)cm from underarm, end with a RS row.

Work 5 rows in garter st (k every row), end with a WS row. Bind off all sts knitwise.

FINISHING

Block pieces to measurements.
Sew sleeve seams.

TURTLENECK

With smaller circular needle and RS facing, starting at right shoulder seam, pick up and k 56 (56, 60, 64, 72) sts evenly around neck opening. Work in rnds of k2, p2 rib until turtleneck measures 8"/20.5cm from pick-up row. Bind off in rib. ❈

PICABO STREET
Picabo's cozy snow-motif sweater is perfect for someone who made her name on the slopes.

"Peek" is an apt nickname for Picabo Street, a free-spirited woman who spent much of her life racing down mountain peaks. From the time she was a young girl in Sun Valley, Idaho, Picabo (a Native American word meaning "shining waters") gravitated to speed and competition, often playing with the boys—and beating them. Her bold skiing led her to the U.S. Ski Team at fifteen years of age, to Olympic silver in 1994, and to gold in the 1998 Olympics. Along the way Picabo ruled women's World Cup downhill, becoming the first U.S. woman ever to win the World Cup downhill title in 1995. She repeated that feat in 1996, and snagged the World Championship title as well. Since retiring from ski racing in 2002, Picabo has taken on family life, raising her three sons and splitting her time between Alabama and Park City. She showed she's still got serious grit by competing in the military combat TV show *Stars Earn Stripes*.

SLIPPER SOCKS

An allover Fair Isle pattern makes stockings extra thick–perfect to warm your feet after a day on the slopes.

 Inspired by World Cup freestyle skier K. C. OAKLEY

SIZE
Woman's Medium

KNITTED MEASUREMENTS
• *Upper leg circumference*
  10"/25.5cm

• *Foot circumference*
  8½"/21.5cm

• *Length from cuff to heel*
  13"/33cm

• *Length from heel to toe*
  9"/23cm

MATERIALS
One 5oz/141g skein (each approx 256yd/234m) of Red Heart *Soft Yarn* (acrylic) each in #4600 white (A), #9820 mid blue (B), and #5142 cherry red (C) 〔4〕

One set (4) each sizes 7 and 8 (4.5 and 5mm) double-pointed needles (dpns) *or size to obtain gauge*

Stitch markers and stitch holder

GAUGE
23 sts and 26 rnds = 4"/10cm over Fair Isle pat using size 8 (5mm) needles.
Take time to check gauge.

K2, P2 RIB
(multiple of 4 sts)
RND 1 *K2, p2; rep from * to end.
Rep rnd 1 for k2, p2 rib.

BRAIDED STITCH
RND 1 With yarn at front of work and bringing next color over last st (this twists the yarn as you work), *with A, p1; with B, p1; rep from * to end.
Rep rnd 1 for braided st.

SOCK
With smaller needles and A, cast on 56 sts, distributing evenly over 3 dpns. Join, being careful not to twist sts, and place marker (pm) for beg of rnd. Work in k2, p2 rib for 1½"/4cm.

☀SLIPPER SOCKS

CHART 1

49

30

20

10

1

56 sts

CHART 2

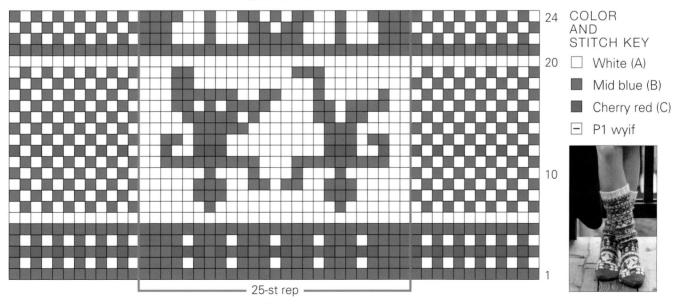

24

20

10

1

25-st rep

49 sts

COLOR AND STITCH KEY

☐ White (A)

▨ Mid blue (B)

▨ Cherry red (C)

⊟ P1 wyif

❋ SLIPPER SOCKS

Change to larger needles.
NEXT RND With A, knit.

BEG CHART 1

Cont in rnds, working chart 1 to end of chart (rnd 65).
RND 66 With A, [k12, ssk] 4 times—52 sts.
RND 67 *With B, k2; with A, k2; rep from * to end of rnd.
RNDS 68–69 *With B, k2; with A, p2; rep from * to end of rnd.
RND 70 *With B, k2; with C, p2; rep from * to end of rnd.
RND 71 *With B, k2; with A, k2; rep from * to end of rnd.
RNDS 72–73 *With B, k2; with A, p2; rep from * to end of rnd.
RND 74 With A, [k11, k2tog] 4 times—48 sts.
Change to smaller needles.

HEEL FLAP

NOTE Heel flap is worked back and forth on the first 12 and last 12 sts of the rnd. Rem 24 sts are on hold. Cont with B only.
NEXT ROW (RS) K12, turn.
NEXT ROW (WS) Sl 1, p23, turn—24 sts.
NEXT ROW (RS) [Sl 1, k1] 12 times, turn.
Rep last 2 rows 7 times more, end with a RS row.

TURN HEEL

ROW 1 (RS) Sl 1, p13, p2tog, p1, turn.
ROW 2 Sl 1, k5, ssk, k1, turn.
ROW 3 Sl 1, p6, p2tog, p1, turn.
ROW 4 Sl 1, k7, ssk, k1, turn.
ROW 5 Sl 1, p8, p2tog, p1, turn.
ROW 6 Sl 1, k9, ssk, k1, turn.
ROW 7 Sl 1, p10, p2tog, p1, turn.
ROW 8 Sl 1, k11, ssk, k1, turn.
ROW 9 Sl 1, p12, p2tog, turn.
Change to larger needles.

GUSSET

NEXT RND With B, sl 1, k 6 heel sts, pm for new beg of rnd, with 1st dpn, k6, ssk, pick up and k 8 sts along heel flap edge, with 2nd dpn, k 24 instep sts, with 3rd dpn, pick up and k 8 sts along heel flap edge, k 7 heel sts—54 sts.
RND 1 With A, k to last 3 sts on 1st dpn, k2tog, k1; on 2nd dpn, k12, M1, k12; on 3rd dpn, k1, ssk, k to end of rnd—52 sts.
RND 2 *With A, k1; with B, k1; rep from * to last st, with A, k1.
RND 3 With A, k to last 3 sts on 1st dpn, k2tog, k1, on 2nd dpn, k25, on 3rd dpn, k1, ssk, k to end of rnd—50 sts.
RND 4 *With B, k1; with A, k1; rep from * to last st, with B, k1.
RND 5 With A, k all sts on 1st dpn, on 2nd dpn, k25, on 3rd dpn, k1, ssk, k to end of rnd—49 sts.

BEG CHART 2

Cont in rnds, working chart 2 to end of chart (rnd 24). Change to smaller needles and cont with B only.

TOE

RND 1 (DEC) K to last 3 sts on 1st dpn, k2tog, k1; on 2nd dpn, k1, ssk, k8, k2tog, k9, k2tog, k1; on 3rd dpn, k1, ssk, k to end of rnd—44 sts.
RND 2 Knit.
RND 3 (DEC) K to last 3 sts on 1st dpn, k2tog, k1; on 2nd dpn, k1, ssk, k to last 3 sts, k2tog, k1; on 3rd dpn, k1, ssk, k to end of rnd—40 sts.
RND 4 Knit.
Rep last 2 rnds 7 times more—12 sts.
With 3rd dpn, k sts from 1st dpn—6 sts on each of 2 dpns. Break yarn.

FINISHING

Graft toe together. Block lightly to measurements. ❋

K. C. OAKLEY

Says K.C., "I am attracted to bright colors and unique patterns, and these slipper socks show off both. They keep my toes warm during the winter and are especially comfortable to put on after taking off my ski boots."

K. C. Oakley, a onetime "weekend warrior" from Piedmont, California, is now a full-time threat on the freestyle moguls tour. K. C. joined Tahoe's Alpine Meadows Freestyle Team at thirteen; by seventeen all her energy was focused on the bumps. In 2011, the overall NorAm title and a silver at the U.S. National Championships landed her on the U.S. Ski Team. With seven World Cup top-ten results, K. C. was named the 2012 FIS World Cup Rookie of the Year and won a spot on the A team. Her goals are clear: "Ski better, ski faster, jump bigger." K. C. also earned a psychology degree at UC Berkeley and is pursuing an MBA. Her foundation, Jill's Legacy, raises funds for lung cancer research in honor of her friend Jill Costello, who died in 2010.

DESIGNED BY KRISTEN ASHBAUGH HELMREICH

PERSONALIZED HEADBAND

Warm your ears in style with your favorite phrase on a double-knit headband—ours salutes ski mecca Squaw Valley.

 Inspired by Olympic alpine skiing medalist JULIA MANCUSO

KNITTED MEASUREMENTS
• *Circumference*
  19½"/49.5cm

• *Width*
  3¼"/8cm

MATERIALS
1 1¾oz/50g ball (each approx
  174yd/160m) of Rowan
  Pure Wool 4 Ply (superwash wool)
  each in #410 indigo (A), #436 kiss
  (B), and #412 snow (C)

One each sizes 1 and 2 (2.25 and
  2.75mm) circular needle,
  16"/40.5cm long, *or size to
  obtain gauge*

Scrap yarn

Stitch marker

Tapestry needle

GAUGE
27 sts and 40 rnds = 4"/10cm
over chart pat using size 2
(2.75mm) needles.
Take time to check gauge.

STITCH GLOSSARY
KFB Knit into the front and back of
next st—1 st increased.

HEADBAND
With smaller needle and A, cast on
132 sts. Join to work in the rnd,
being careful not to twist sts, and
place marker for beg of rnd.

NEXT (INC) RND Kfb to end of
rnd—264 sts.

DIVIDE FOR FRONT AND BACK
NEXT (2-COLOR) RND Join B, *k1
with A for front of headband, bring
both strands forward, p1 with B for
back of headband, bring both

✳PERSONALIZED HEADBAND

CHART 2

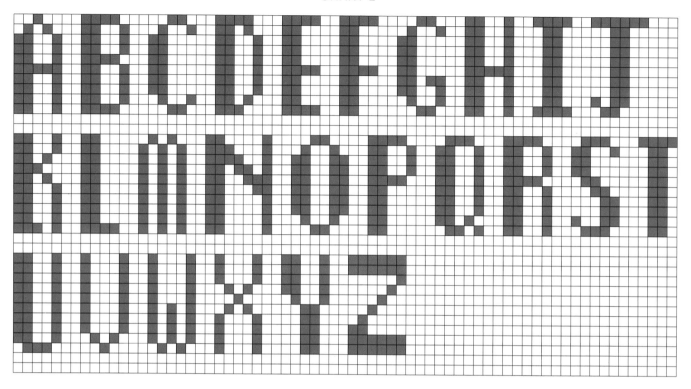

COLOR KEY

- ■ Indigo (A)
- ■ Kiss (B)
- □ Snow (C)

CHART 1

24
20
10
1

4-st
rep

strands back; rep from * to end
of rnd.
Rep last rnd once more—132 sts in
A for front of headband, 132 sts
in B for back.
Slip all B sts to scrap yarn to be
worked later for back—132 sts in A
rem on needle.

BEG CHARTS
RND 1 With larger needle, A and C,
beg working chart 1 from right to left,
repeating to end of rnd. If desired,
beginning on rnd 8 of chart, work
desired intarsia pattern using chart 2
(sample says "SQUAW VALLEY
USA"). Work even until 24 rows of
chart have been worked. Leave
these sts on larger needle to be
worked later; break C.

BACK
Sl 132 sts in B from scrap
yarn to smaller needle.

BEG STRIPE PAT
[With C, knit 3 rnds; with A,
knit 3 rnds; with B, knit 3 rnds]
3 times. Break B.

JOIN FRONT AND BACK
With WS of front and back held tog
and front of band facing, using A
and C, work 2-color rnd twice
around with smaller needle—264 sts.
Break C.
NEXT (DEC) RND With A, ssk to end
of rnd—132 sts. Bind off.

FINISHING
Block lightly to measurements. ✳

82

JULIA MANCUSO
Indoors or out, style-setter Julia rocks slouchy knit hats and always appreciates timeless retro looks like this headband.

Save yourself some time and don't ask what Julia Mancuso can do. Instead, ask what she can't do. Squaw Valley–bred "Super Jules" broke onto the World Cup circuit at age fifteen, competed in the Olympics at age seventeen, set a U.S. record for Junior World Championships medals (five gold, three bronze), and started her twenties by capturing two World Championships medals. She went on to win gold in her second Olympics and two silvers in her third. Her running tally of five World Championships medals proves she is not even close to slowing down. "At this point in my career, I really want to win. I go into every race with the attitude that you have to put it all on the line." In her down time the philanthropist, gym owner, underwear designer, and professional free spirit enjoys surfing, yoga, paddleboarding, and everything about the ocean life at her home away from home in Maui.

SPARKLE SLOUCHY HAT

Glistening metallic thread in a variegated wool-blend
yarn makes a broken-rib hat extra special.

Inspired by Olympic and X Games snowboarding medalist LINDSEY JACOBELLIS

SIZE
Instructions are written for size
Medium.

KNITTED MEASUREMENTS
• *Brim circumference
(slightly stretched)*
18"/45.5cm

• *Length*
10½"/26.5cm

MATERIALS
1 2½oz/70g ball (each approx
153yd/140m) of Red Heart
Boutique Midnight
(acrylic/wool/nylon/metallic
polyester) in #1937 moonlight OR
#1942 serenade

One each sizes 7 and 9
(4.5 and 5.5mm) circular needle,
16"/40cm long, *or size to
obtain gauge*

One set (5) size 9 (5.5mm)
double-pointed needles (dpns)

Stitch marker

Tapestry needle

GAUGE
18 sts and 25 rnds = 4"/10 cm
over broken rib using size 9
(5.5mm) needles.
Take time to check gauge.

K1, P1 RIB
(over an even number of sts)
RND 1 *K1, p1; rep from * to end
of rnd.
Rep rnd 1 for k1, p1 rib.

BROKEN RIB
(over an even number of sts)
RND 1 *K1, p1; rep from * to end
of rnd.
RND 2 Knit.
Rep rnds 1 and 2 for broken rib.

NOTE
Change to dpns when there
are too few sts to fit comfortably
on circular needle.

HAT
With smaller circular needle, cast on
90 sts. Join to work in the rnd, being
careful not to twist sts, and place
marker for beg of rnd. Work in k1, p1
rib for 4"/10cm.
Change to larger circular needle and
work in broken rib until hat measures
9¾"/25cm from beg.

CROWN SHAPING
RND 1 *Ssk; rep from * to
end of rnd—45 sts.
RND 2 Knit.
RND 3 *Ssk; rep from * to last st,
k1—23 sts.
RND 4 Knit.
RND 5 *Ssk; rep from * to last st,
k1—12 sts.
RND 6 *Ssk; rep from * to end of
rnd—6 sts.
Break yarn, leaving a long tail.
Thread tail through rem sts and pull
tightly to secure.

FINISHING
Block lightly to measurements.

❊ SPARKLE SLOUCHY HAT

LINDSEY JACOBELLIS
Lindsey's a knitter and loves to make cool hats like this one (but not bathing suits—that was a bad experiment!).

❊ Lindsey Jacobellis is one of the many winter athletes who knit. See Olympian Edie Thys Morgan's essay "Close Knit" (page 19) for a glimpse into how important knitting was to Edie and her fellow U.S. Ski Team members, both as an outlet for expressing their creativity and as a way to connect with family, friends, and each other while on the road.

Lindsey Jacobellis likes fashion, and collecting shoes, and glittery things—like gold medals. Perhaps that's why she is the most decorated woman in the sport of snowboard cross, with twenty-four SBX World Cup wins, an Olympic silver medal, and a record seven X Games golds. Big brother Benny introduced "Lucky" Lindsey to riding when she was eleven, in the mountains of Vermont. A few years later, the Connecticut native moved to Vermont and enrolled at Stratton Mountain School, where she could ride every day. A regular on the circuit since 2003, Lindsey has dominated the sport, though back-to-back knee surgeries kept her sidelined for half of 2012 and all of 2013. Determination and many hours a day rehabbing at the U.S. Ski Team Center of Excellence ensure that she will be back in action for 2014. When she's not riding or training, Lindsey likes to hang out with friends and surf (especially in Fiji).

CABLE & GARTER BLANKET

Nothing's cozier than a cabled blanket, especially one knit in a sumptuous bulky merino-mohair blend.

 Inspired by Olympic medalist in freestyle skiing SHANNON BAHRKE HAPPE

KNITTED MEASUREMENTS

- *Width*
  45½"/115.5cm

- *Length*
  67"/170cm

MATERIALS

8 3½oz/100g skeins (each approx 126yd/115m) of Rowan *Cocoon* (merino/mohair) each in #803 scree (A) and #802 alpine (B)

5 skeins in #811 lavender ice (C)

Size 10½ (7mm) circular needle, 32"/80cm long, *or size to obtain gauge*

One pair size 10½ (7mm) needles

Stitch holders

Cable needle (cn)

GAUGE

13 sts and 26 rows = 4"/10cm over garter st using size 10½ (7mm) needles.
Take time to check gauge.

STITCH GLOSSARY

3-ST RPC Sl 1 to cn and hold to *back*, k2, p1 from cn.
3-ST LPC Sl 2 to cn and hold to *front*, p1, k2 from cn.
4-ST RPC Sl 2 to cn and hold to *back*, k2, p2 from cn.
4-ST LPC Sl 2 to cn and hold to *front*, p2, k2 from cn.
4-ST RC Sl 2 to cn and hold to *back*, k2, k2 from cn.
4-ST LC Sl 2 to cn and hold to *front*, k2, k2 from cn.
9-ST LPC Sl 5 to cn and hold to *front*, k4, sl center p st from cn to LH needle and purl it, k4 from cn.
12-ST RC Sl 8 to cn and hold to *back*, k4, sl last 4 sts from cn to LH needle and k4, k4 from cn.
12-ST LC Sl 8 to cn and hold to *front*, sl last 4 sts from cn to LH needle and k4, k4 from cn.

NOTES

1) Blanket is worked in strips and sewn together, and then borders are worked and sewn to blanket.
2) The stitch count on cable strip 1 starts at 37 sts, increases to 45 sts, and then decreases to 37 sts.
3) Circular needle is used to accommodate large number of stitches. Do *not* join.

✳CABLE & GARTER BLANKET

STITCH KEY

- ☐ K on RS, P on WS
- ⊟ P on RS, K on WS
- ◻ K2tog
- ◹ P2tog
- ◿ P3tog
- ◻ Ssk
- Ⓜ M1
- ▱ 3-st RPC
- ▱ 3-st LPC
- ▱ 4-st RPC
- ▱ 4-st LPC
- ▱ 4-st RC
- ▱ 4-st LC
- ▱ 9-st LPC
- ▱ 12-st RC
- ▱ 12-st LC

CHART 1

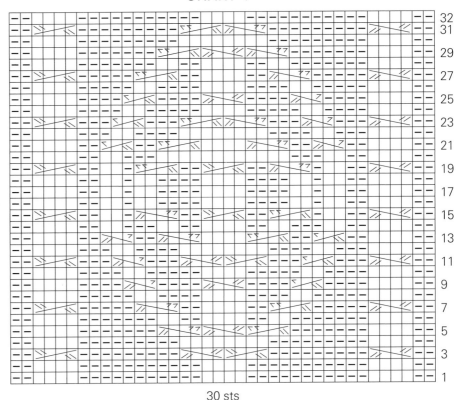

30 sts

CHART 2

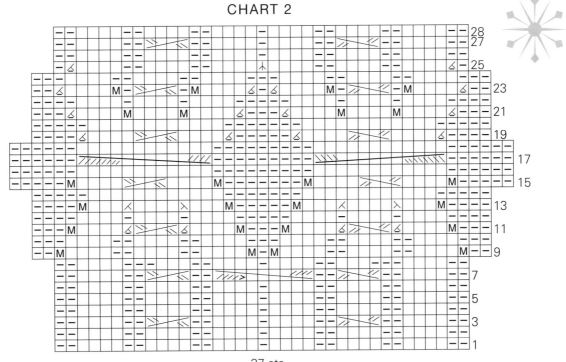

37 sts

❄CABLE & GARTER BLANKET

CABLE STRIP 1 (MAKE 2)
With straight needles and A,
cast on 38 sts.
ROW 1 (RS) P2, k4, p11, k4,
p11, k4, p2.
ROW 2 K2, p4, k11, p4, k11, p4, k2.
Starting with row 1 of chart 1, rep
rows 1–32 of chart until piece
measures 59"/150cm from beg, end
with a WS row. Bind off in pat.

CABLE STRIP 2 (MAKE 1)
With straight needles and C, cast on
37 sts. Starting with row 1 of chart 2,
rep rows 1–28 of chart until piece
measures 59"/150cm from beg, end
with a WS row. Bind off in pat.

GARTER STRIPE PANEL (MAKE 2)
With straight needles and C,
cast on 27 sts.
ROW 1 (RS) With C, knit.
ROW 2 Knit.
ROWS 3 AND 4 With B, knit.
ROWS 5 AND 6 With A, knit.
ROWS 7 AND 8 With B, knit.
Rep rows 1–8 until piece measures
59"/150cm from beg, end with
a WS row. Bind off in pat.

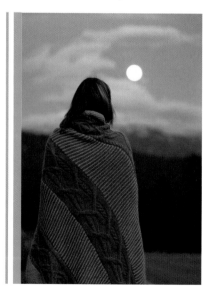

FINISHING
Block strips lightly. Working from
left to right, sew strips together in the
following sequence: cable panel 1,
garter stripe panel, cable panel 2,
garter stripe panel, cable panel 1.

BOTTOM BORDER
With circular needle and B, cast on
161 sts.
Work in garter st (knit every row) until
piece measures 4"/10cm from beg,
end with a WS row.

RIGHT BORDER
NEXT ROW (RS) K14 and place
these sts onto holder for left side
border, bind off next 133 sts, knit rem
14 sts for right side border.
Working on 14 sts for right side
border only, cont in garter st until
piece measures 59"/150cm from
beg, end with a WS row. Break yarn
and place sts on holder.

LEFT BORDER
Place 14 sts from left side border
holder on needle, ready for a WS
row. Join B and cont in garter st until
piece measures 59"/150cm from
beg, end with a WS row.

TOP BORDER
NEXT (JOINING) ROW (RS) K14 from
left side border, cast on 133 sts and
k14 from right side border holder—
161 sts. Cont in garter st until piece
measures 4"/10cm from joining row,
end with a WS row. Bind off all sts.

With RS facing, lay bottom border
against bottom edge of joined strips
and pin in place.
Pin side borders to sides of blanket,
then pin top border to top of joined
strips. Sew neatly in place using
mattress stitch. Gently press seams
and block lightly to measurements. ❄

SHANNON BAHRKE HAPPE
Shannon treasures the
blanket made for her
by Grandma Bahrke, who
taught her to be a strong,
independent woman and
to follow her dreams.
"Every time I snuggle up
with it I think of what an
amazing woman she was."

When Shannon Bahrke was
twelve, some saw her as an
unruly young girl. The coach of
the Squaw Valley Freestyle Team
saw potential, and cultivated the
talents that led Shannon to move
to Salt Lake City to pursue her
dream of making the U.S. Ski
Team. She went on to compete in
six World Championships and
three Olympics, earning two
Olympic medals, seven World
Cup wins and one overall title,
and six national titles. Shannon's
brother, Scotty, followed in her
tracks and is a world-class
freestyle aerialist. In 2007 she
and her husband, Matt, started
the Silver Bean Coffee Co., which
benefits the U.S. Ski Team and
various charities. Shannon can
also be found hiking, biking,
golfing, riding motorcycles,
practicing yoga, reading, or
racing cars at the track.

WHIMSICAL SKI HAT

Brighten up your winter wardrobe with a Fair Isle hat that's bursting with color and topped by a pair of pompoms.

 Inspired by Olympic champion alpine skier DEBBIE ARMSTRONG

SIZES
Instructions are written for size Small. Changes for Medium and Large are in parentheses. (Shown in size Small.)

KNITTED MEASUREMENTS
• *Brim circumference (slightly stretched)*
18 (20, 22)"/45.5 (51, 56)cm

• *Length*
8 (8¾, 9½)"/20.5 (22, 24)cm

MATERIALS
1 7oz/198g skein (each approx 370yd/338m) of Red Heart *With Love* (acrylic) each in #1814 true blue (A), #1502 iced aqua (B), #1703 candy pink (C), #1701 hot pink (D), #1252 mango (E), and #1907 boysenberry (F) (**4**)

Size 9 (5.5mm) circular needle, 16"/40cm long, *or size to obtain gauge*

Stitch marker

Pompom maker (optional)

GAUGE
16 sts and 20 rows = 4"/10cm over Fair Isle pat using size 9 (5.5mm) needles.
Take time to check gauge.

3-NEEDLE BIND-OFF
1) Hold right sides of pieces together on two needles. Insert 3rd needle knitwise into 1st st of each needle, and wrap yarn knitwise.
2) Knit these 2 sts together, and slip them off the needles. *Knit the next 2 sts together in the same manner.
3) Slip 1st st on 3rd needle over 2nd st and off needle. Rep from * in step 2 across row until all sts are bound off.

❋WHIMSICAL SKI HAT

K2, P2 RIB
(multiple of 4 sts)
RND 1 *K2, p2; rep from
* to end of rnd.
Rep rnd 1 for k2, p2 rib.

HAT
With A, cast on 68 (76, 84) sts. Join to work in the rnd, being careful not to twist sts, and place marker (pm) for beg of rnd. Work in k2, p2 rib for 1½"/4cm. Break A and join B.
RND 1 (INC) With B, knit, inc 2 (4, 6) sts evenly around—70 (80, 90) sts.
RND 2 Purl. Break B and join F.
RND 3 With F, knit.
RND 4 Purl. Break F and join D.
With D, knit 2 (3, 4) rnds.

BEG CHART 1
NEXT RND Continuing in St st, work 10-st rep of chart 1 a total of 7 (8, 9) times.
Cont in pat as established through chart rnd 8.
With D, knit 2 (3, 4) rnds.
Break D and join F.
NEXT RND With F, knit.

NEXT RND Purl. Break F and join C.
NEXT RND With C, knit.
NEXT RND Purl. Break C and join B.
With B, knit 2 (3, 4) rnds.

BEG CHART 2
NEXT RND Continuing in St st, work 10-st rep of chart 2 a total of 7 (8, 9) times.
Cont in pat as established through chart rnd 8.
With B, knit 2 (3, 4) rnds.
Break B and join C.
NEXT RND With C, knit.
NEXT RND Purl. Break C and join D.
NEXT RND With D, knit.

FINISHING
Bring ends of circular needle together and, with spare needle, use 3-needle bind-off to join top of hat.

POMPOMS (MAKE 2)
With A and B held together, make a pompom 2½"/6.5cm in diameter. Attach one pompom to each corner of top of hat.❋

DEBBIE ARMSTRONG
Debbie's fun, brightly colored hat is patterned after the one she wore on her way to gold in Sarajevo.

Growing up in Seattle as the child of two teachers, Debbie Armstrong embraced education, the outdoors, and all sports. But ultimately she chose skiing. Debbie won the first training run of her first World Cup downhill, and went on to Olympic gold in Sarajevo in 1984. She retired from competition in 1988 but stayed in the ski world as the only U.S. Ski Team member to become a Professional Ski Instructors of America Alpine Team member. What does she love about her job? "Making a difference on the hill—making people happy, teaching them something, challenging them, exciting them." Debbie and her daughter live in Colorado's "Ski Town, U.S.A.," where Debbie is alpine competitive program director for the Steamboat Springs Winter Sports Club and is involved in various charitable causes, including the SKIFORALL Foundation, which opens skiing events to the disabled.

CHART 1

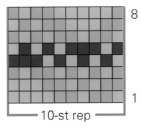

8

1

—10-st rep—

COLOR KEY

- ■ True blue (A)
- ■ Blue Hawaii (B)
- ■ Candy pink (C)
- ■ Hot pink (D)
- ■ Mango (E)

CHART 2

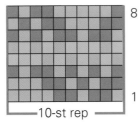

8

1

—10-st rep—

SPIDER BLANKET

Warm up and stay cool wrapped in this generous-size blanket with a striking duplicate-stitch spider motif.

 Inspired by Olympic champion alpine skier TOMMY MOE

KNITTED MEASUREMENTS
• *Width* 54"/137cm

• *Length* 60"/152.5cm

MATERIALS
12 5oz/141g skeins (each approx 256yd/234m) of Red Heart *Soft Yarn* (acrylic) in #9440 light grey heather ▪

2 skeins in #4614 black (CC)

Size 11 (8mm) circular needle, 32"/80cm long, *or size to obtain gauge*

GAUGE
12 sts and 16 rows = 4"/10cm over St st with yarn held double using size 11 (8mm) needles. *Take time to check gauge.*

SEED STITCH
(over an even number of sts)
ROW 1 (RS) *K1, p1; rep from * to end.
ROW 2 K the purl and p the knit sts. Rep row 2 for seed st.

NOTES
1) Blanket is worked back and forth in rows; circular needle is used to accommodate large number of sts. Do *not* join.
2) Two strands of yarn are held together throughout.
3) Spider motif is worked in duplicate stitch after blanket is knitted.

BLANKET
With 2 strands of MC held together, cast on 156 sts. Work 8 rows in seed st, end with a WS row.

LOWER BLOCK SECTION
ROW 1 (RS) Work seed st over first 6 sts, [k36, p36] twice, work seed st over last 6 sts.
Rep row 1 for a total of 48 rows, end with a WS row.

CENTER BLOCK SECTION 1
NEXT ROW (RS) Work seed st over first 6 sts, p36, work seed st over next 72 sts, k36, work in seed st over last 6 sts.
Rep last row 3 times more, end with a WS row.

ROW 1 (RS) Work seed st over first 6 sts, p36, work seed st over next 4 sts, k64, work seed st over next 4 sts, k36, work seed st over last 6 sts.
ROW 2 Work seed st over first 6 sts, p36, work seed st over next 4 sts, p64, work seed st over next 4 sts, k36, work seed st over last 6 sts.
Rep last 2 rows 21 times more, end with a WS row.

CENTER BLOCK SECTION 2
ROW 1 (RS) Work seed st over first 6 sts, k36, work seed st over next 4 sts, k64, work seed st over next 4 sts, p36, work seed st over last 6 sts.
ROW 2 Work seed st over first 6 sts, k36, work seed st over next 4 sts, p64, work seed st over next 4 sts, p36, work seed st over last 6 sts.
Rep last 2 rows 23 times more, end with a WS row.

CENTER BLOCK SECTION 3
ROW 1 (RS) Work seed st over first 6 sts, p36, work seed st over next 4 sts, k64, work seed st over next 4 sts, k36, work seed st over last 6 sts.

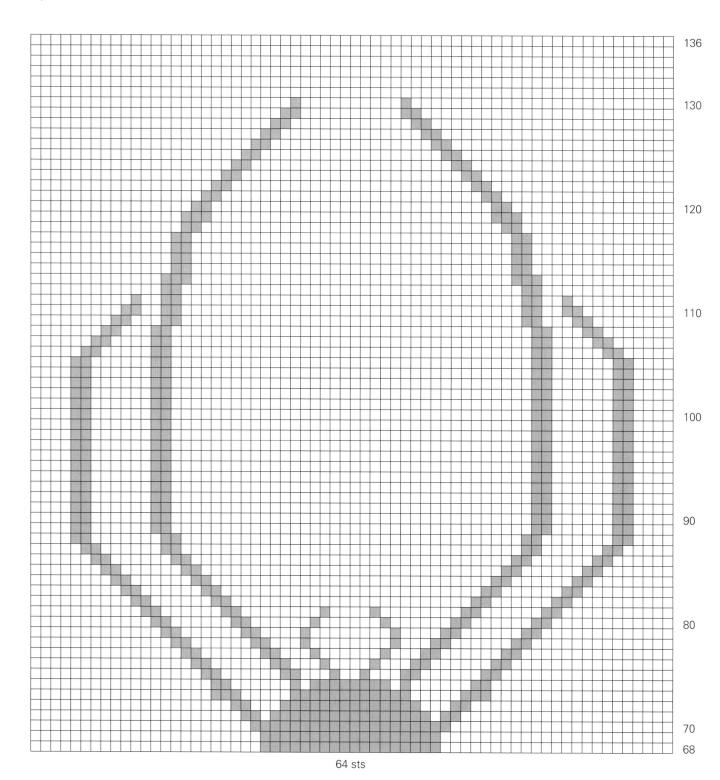

136

130

120

110

100

90

80

70
68

64 sts

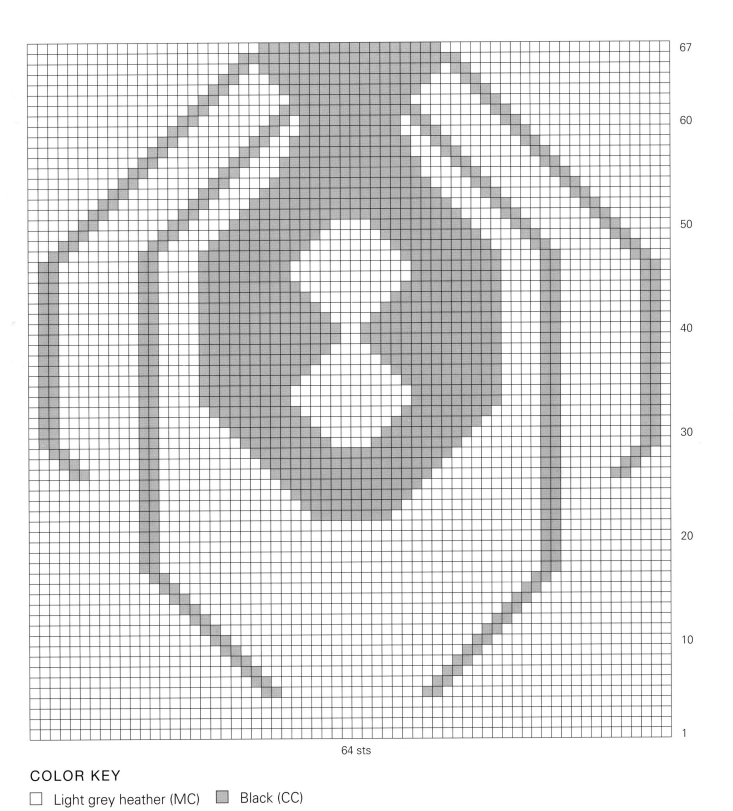

67

60

50

40

30

20

10

1

64 sts

COLOR KEY

☐ Light grey heather (MC) ▨ Black (CC)

✳SPIDER BLANKET

TOMMY MOE
In honor of fun-loving Tommy's long-running relationships with ski apparel company Spyder and cold climates, we created this big, cozy blanket adorned with a spider.

ROW 2 Work seed st over first 6 sts, p36, work seed st over next 4 sts, p64, work seed st over next 4 sts, k36, work seed st over last 6 sts. Rep last 2 rows 21 times more, end with a WS row.
NEXT ROW (RS) Work seed st over first 6 sts, p36, work seed st over next 72 sts, k36, work seed st over last 6 sts.
Rep last row 3 times more, end with a WS row.

UPPER BLOCK SECTION
ROW 1 (RS) Work seed st over first 6 sts, [k36, p36] twice, work seed st over last 6 sts.
Rep row 1 for a total of 48 rows, end with a WS row.
Work 8 rows in seed st across all sts. Bind off in pat.

FINISHING
With 2 strands of CC held together, work spider in duplicate stitch over center 64 sts of blanket, following chart for stitch placement. Block lightly to measurements. ✳

When it comes to all-time mountain men, three-time Olympian Tommy Moe has to be part of the conversation. The Montana native of Norwegian heritage refined his skills in Alaska and made the U.S. Ski Team at age sixteen. In 1994 in Lillehammer, Tommy became the first American male skier to win two medals (downhill gold, super-G silver) in one Olympics, securing his status as a skiing legend. After retiring in 1998, Tommy settled in Jackson Hole, Wyoming, with his wife, Megan (U.S. Ski Team alum and Olympian), and their two daughters. In summers he leads the popular Cast & Carve heli-skiing and fishing tours out of Tordrillo Mountain Lodge in Alaska, which he co-owns. Whether skiing, fishing, or running rivers, the mighty, mellow Moe inspires outdoor enthusiasts of all ages.

DESIGNED BY GRACE AKHREM

SLIP STITCH BEANIE

A two-color slip stitch pattern and a simple shape
are perfect for a cap that shows off your team colors.

 Inspired by Olympic freestyle skier SCOTTY BAHRKE

SIZE
Adult Medium

KNITTED MEASUREMENTS
• *Brim circumference*
  20½"/52cm

• *Length*
  9"/23cm

MATERIALS
1 1¾oz/50g ball (each approx
191yd/175m) of Rowan *Felted
Tweed DK* (merino/alpaca/viscose)
each in #154 ginger (MC) and
#177 clay (CC) OR 1 ball
each in #158 pine (MC) and
#181 mineral (CC) ③

Size 4 (3.5mm) circular needle,
16"/40cm long, *or size to
obtain gauge*

One set (5) size 4 (3.5mm)
double-pointed needles (dpns)

Stitch marker

GAUGE
22 sts and 24 rnds = 4"/10cm
over sl stitch pat (blocked) using size
4 (3.5mm) needles.
Take time to check gauge.

GARTER STITCH
(worked in the round)
RND 1 Knit.
RND 2 Purl.
Rep rnds 1 and 2 for garter st.

SLIP STITCH PATTERN
(multiple of 4 sts)
RND 1 With CC, knit.
RNDS 2–4 With MC, *k3, sl 1;
rep from * to end of rnd.
RND 5 With CC, knit.
RND 6 With MC, knit.
RNDS 7–9 With CC, k1, sl 1, *k3, sl
1; rep from * to last 2 sts, k2.
RND 10 With MC, knit.
Rep rnds 1–10 for slip st pat.

❋ SLIP STITCH BEANIE

NOTES

1) Change to dpns when there are too few sts to fit comfortably on circular needle.

2) Slip all sts purlwise with yarn in back.

3) When changing colors, carry yarn up the inside of work; do not break yarn until specified.

BEANIE

With circular needle and MC, cast on 112 sts. Join to work in the rnd, being careful not to twist sts, place marker (pm) for beg of rnd. Work 6 rnds in garter st.

Beg working in slip st pat, starting with rnd 1, working 10-row rep 5 times, then rnds 1–7 once more.

CROWN SHAPING

RND 1 With CC, k1, sl 1, *ssk, k1, sl 1; rep from * to last 2 sts, ssk, remove marker, k1 from next rnd, pm—84 sts.

RND 2 With CC, *sl 1, k2tog; rep from * to end of rnd—56 sts.

RND 3 With MC, knit.

RND 4 With CC, knit.

RNDS 5–8 With MC, *k1, sl 1; rep from * to end of rnd.

RND 9 With CC, knit.

RND 10 With MC, *k2, k2tog; rep from * to end of rnd—42 sts.

RND 11 With CC, *sl 1, k2tog; rep from * to end of rnd—28 sts.

RND 1 With MC, *sl 1, k1; rep from * to end of rnd. Break CC.

RND 13 With MC, knit.

RNDS 14 AND 15 *Ssk; rep from * to end of rnd—7 sts. Break yarn, leaving a long tail. Thread tail through rem sts and pull tightly to secure.

FINISHING

Block lightly to measurements. ❋

SCOTTY BAHRKE
Scotty is a big fan of the Green Bay Packers, so of course his beanie had to be green and yellow. But you can make it in the colors of your own favorite team!

Scotty Bahrke started off following in his sister Shannon's footsteps, but then he took off in a different direction—straight up. Until 2005 the Tahoe City, California, native and Squaw Valley Freestyle Team star was a triple threat, in moguls, aerials, and big air. But when he qualified for the World Cup in aerials and went on to win the 2005 NorAm title, he realized his future was, quite literally, up in the air. After focusing on aerials, he competed in the World Championships in 2007 and 2009. Then in 2010, while in Vancouver to root for his big sister at the Olympics, he was named to the team himself just five days before the competition, replacing a teammate who was ill. His first World Cup podium came in 2011 and his first victory in 2012. The toughest part of his sport? "Knowing you're going to crash big once or twice a year, but not knowing when it's coming."

SLOUCHY SOCKS

Warm up chilled feet with a wool and alpaca blend in a pattern that evokes fresh ski tracks.

 Inspired by Olympic snowboarder ELENA HIGHT

SIZE

Instructions are written for women's size Medium.

KNITTED MEASUREMENTS

- Upper leg circumference (slightly stretched) 10"/25.5cm

- Foot circumference (slightly stretched) 8"/20.5cm

- Length from cuff to heel 15"/38cm

- Length from heel to toe 9"/23cm

MATERIALS

4 1¾oz/50g balls (each approx 95yd/87m) of Rowan *Felted Tweed Aran* (merino/alpaca/viscose) in #720 pebble (4)

One set (4) size 6 (4mm) double-pointed needles (dpns) *or size to obtain gauge*

Stitch markers

GAUGE

20 sts and 32 rnds = 4"/10cm over St st using size 6 (4mm) needles. *Take time to check gauge.*

SOCKS (MAKE 2)

Cast on 48 sts and divide evenly over 3 dpns. Join to work in the rnd, being careful not to twist sts, and place marker (pm) for beg of rnd.
RNDS 1–9 *P1, k4, p1; rep from * to end of rnd.
RND 10 *P1, k4, M1, p1; rep from * to end of rnd—56 sts.

LEG SHAPING

RND 11 *P1, k5, p1; rep from * to end of rnd.
RND 12 *P1, k2tog, k3, M1, p1; rep from * to end of rnd.
Rep last 2 rnds 3 times more.
RNDS 19–21 *P1, k5, p1; rep from * to end of rnd.
RND 22 *P1, M1, k3, ssk, p1; rep from * to end of rnd.
RND 23 *P1, k5, p1; rep from * to end of rnd.
Rep last 2 rnds 3 times more.
RND 30 *P1, k5, p1; rep from * to end of rnd.
Rep rnds 11–30 once more.
RND 51 *P1, k5, p1; rep from * to end of rnd.
RND 52 *P1, k2tog, k3, p1; rep from * to end of rnd—48 sts.
RND 53 *P1, k4, p1; rep from * to end of rnd.
RND 54 *P1, k2tog, k2, M1, p1; rep from * to end of rnd.
Rep last 2 rnds 3 times more.

RNDS 61–63 *P1, k4, p1; rep from * to end of rnd.
RND 64 *P1, M1, k2, ssk, p1; rep from * to end of rnd.
RND 65 *P1, k4, p1; rep from * to end of rnd.
Rep last 2 rnds 3 times more.
RNDS 72 AND 73 *P1, k4, p1; rep from * to end of rnd.
RND 74 *P1, k2tog, k2, p1; rep from * to end of rnd—40 sts.
RND 75 *P1, k3, p1; rep from * to end of rnd.
RND 76 *P1, k2tog, k1, M1, p1; rep from * to end of rnd.
Rep last 2 rnds 3 times more.
RNDS 83–85 *P1, k3, p1; rep from * to end of rnd.
RND 86 *P1, M1, k1, ssk, p1; rep from * to end of rnd.
RND 87 *P1, k3, p1; rep from * to end of rnd.
Rep last 2 rnds 3 times more.
RNDS 94–101 *P1, k3, p1; rep from * to end of rnd.

HEEL FLAP

NOTE Heel flap is worked back and forth on the first 10 and last 10 sts of the rnd. Rem 20 sts are on hold.
ROW 1 (RS) Sl 1, [k3, p2] twice, turn.
ROW 2 (WS) Sl 1, [p3, k2] 3 times, p3, k1, turn—20 sts.
ROW 3 (RS) Sl 1, [k3, p2] 3 times, k3, p1 times, turn.
ROW 4 (WS) Sl 1, [p3, k2] 3 times, p3, k1, turn.
Rep last 4 rows 8 times more, end with a WS row.

✳SLOUCHY SOCKS

TURN HEEL

ROW 1 (RS) Sl 1, k10, ssk, k1, turn.
ROW 2 (WS) Sl 1, p3, p2tog, p1, turn.
ROW 3 Sl 1, k4, ssk, k1, turn.
ROW 4 Sl 1, p5, p2tog, p1, turn.
Cont in this manner, working
1 more st before the dec in each row, until 12 sts rem for heel, end with a WS row.

GUSSET

NEXT RND Sl 1, k 5 heel sts, pm for new beg of rnd, with dpn #1, knit rem 6 heel sts, pick up and k 10 sts along heel flap edge; with dpn #2, k 20 instep sts; with dpn #3, pick up and k 10 sts along heel flap edge, k 6 heel sts—52 sts.
RND 1 K to last 3 sts on dpn #1, k2tog, k1; on dpn #2, p1, [k3, p2] 3 times, k3, p1; on dpn #3, k1, ssk, k to end of rnd—50 sts.
RND 2 K sts on dpn #1; on dpn #2, p1, [k3, p2] 3 times, k3, p1; k sts on dpn #3.

Rep last 2 rnds 5 times more—40 sts.
Work even in pat until sock measures 7½"/19cm from back of heel, or 1½"/4cm less than desired length of finished foot from heel to toe.

TOE

RND 1 (DEC) K to last 3 sts on dpn #1, k2tog, k1; on dpn #2, k1, ssk, k to last 3 instep sts, k2tog, k1; on dpn #3, k1, ssk, k to end of rnd—36 sts.
RND 2 Knit.
Rep last 2 rnds 6 times more—12 sts.
With dpn #3, k sts from dpn #1—6 sts on each of 2 dpns. Break yarn, leaving a long tail.

FINISHING

Graft rem sts tog for toe. Block lightly to measurements.✳

ELENA HIGHT

Elena's socks are inspired by a pair her grandmother knitted for her, which she takes everywhere to remind her of her family. "These socks are so warm and cozy, they are the absolute best thing to put on once I have taken my boots off after a long day on the hill."

Hawaii-born Elena Hight saw her first snowboard at Bogus Basin, a small ski resort in Idaho, at the age of six. A year later she was competing on one, and at thirteen she became the first woman to land a 900-degree spin in competition. Soon back-to-back 900s became her signature. In 2006, at just sixteen, Elena went to her first Olympics and placed sixth. In 2010, she joined the U.S. Halfpipe Team for another Olympics, and she has her eye on her third. Since 2006, Elena has stood on nearly a dozen podiums at major events, including the X Games, U.S. Grand Prix, and more. She continues to raise the bar in snowboarding, becoming the first man or woman to land a double backside alley-oop rodeo in a halfpipe competition.

DESIGNED BY SALLY MELVILLE

PODIUM PULLOVER

Exposed zippers can double as vents in a wool-alpaca knit that's fit for the medal stand—or any special winter moment.

 Inspired by World Cup and Olympic Nordic skier KIKKAN RANDALL

SIZES
Instructions are written for unisex size X-Small. Changes for Small, Medium, Large, and X-Large are in parentheses.
(Shown in size X-Small.)

KNITTED MEASUREMENTS
- *Chest (slightly stretched)*
  33 (37, 41, 45, 49)"/84 (94, 104, 114, 124.5)cm

- *Length*
  25 (25½, 26, 26½, 27)"/63.5 (64.5, 66, 67, 68.5)cm

- *Upper arm*
  12¾ (14, 15½, 16¾, 18)"/32.5 (35.5, 9.5, 42.5, 45.5)cm

MATERIALS
6 (7, 7, 8, 8) 3½ oz/100g balls (each approx 220yd/200m) of Rowan *Creative Focus Worsted* (wool/alpaca) in #402 charcoal heather ④

One pair size 6 (4mm) needles *or size to obtain gauge*

Size 6 (4mm) circular needle, 16"/40cm long

Stitch markers and stitch holders

3 non-separating zippers, each 9"/23cm long

2 non-separating zippers, each 7"/18cm long

GAUGE
24.5 sts and 28 rows = 4"/10 cm over k2, p2 rib (slightly stretched) using size 6 (4mm) needles.
Take time to check gauge.

K2, P2 RIB
(multiple of 4 sts)
ROW 1 (RS) *K2, p2; rep from * to end.
Rep row 1 for k2, p2 rib.

K2, P2 RIB
(multiple of 4 sts plus 2)
ROW 1 (RS) *K2, p2; rep from * to last 2 sts, k2.
ROW 2 *P2, k2; rep from * to last 2 sts, p2.
Rep rows 1 and 2 for k2, p2 rib.

✳ PODIUM PULLOVER

NOTES
1) All zippers are functional except the shoulder zipper, which is purely decorative.
2) Zippers are sewn to RS of garment as a decorative detail.
3) Lower fronts are worked in 2 pieces to accommodate zipper opening, then joined.
4) Sleeves are worked in 2 pieces to accommodate zipper opening, then joined.

BACK
With straight needles, cast on 102 (114, 126, 138, 150) sts. Work in k2, p2 rib for 13 rows, end with a RS row.
NEXT (DEC) ROW (WS) Work in rib for 21 (25, 29, 33, 37) sts, place marker (pm), work in rib for 60 (64, 68, 72, 76) sts, pm, work in rib to end.
NEXT (DEC) ROW (RS) Work in rib to 2 sts before first marker, k2tog, slip marker (sm), work in rib to second marker, sm, ssk, work in rib to end.
NEXT ROW (WS) Work in rib to 1 st before first marker, p1, sm, work in rib to second marker, sm, p1, work in rib to end.
Cont in rib, keeping st before first marker and after second marker as knit on RS rows and purl on WS rows, rep dec row every 8th row 5 times more—90 (102, 114, 126, 138) sts. Work even in rib until piece measures 10"/25.5cm from beg, end with a RS row.
NEXT ROW (WS) Work in rib to first marker, remove marker, p1, pm, work in rib to 1 st before second marker, pm, p1, remove marker, work in rib to end.
NEXT (INC) ROW (RS) Work in rib to first marker, M1, sm, work in rib to

second marker, sm, M1, work in rib to end—92 (104, 116, 128, 140) sts.
Rep inc row every 6th row 5 times more, incorporating inc sts into k2, p2 rib—102 (114, 126, 138, 150) sts. Remove markers and cont even in rib until piece measures 16½"/42cm from beg, end with a WS row.

ARMHOLE SHAPING
Bind off 5 (7, 9, 11, 13) sts at beg of next 2 rows—92 (100, 108, 116, 124) sts.
NEXT (DEC) ROW (RS) K2, ssk, work in rib to last 4 sts, k2tog, k2—90 (98, 106, 114, 122) sts.
NEXT ROW (WS) P3, work in rib to last 3 sts, p3.
Rep last 2 rows 5 (9, 11, 15, 17) times more—80 (80, 84, 84, 88) sts. Keeping first and last 3 sts in St st (k on RS, p on WS), work even until armhole measures 7 (7½, 8, 8½, 9)"/18 (19, 20.5, 21.5, 23)cm, end with a WS row.

SHOULDER SHAPING
Bind off 4 sts at beg of next 8 (8, 6, 6, 2) rows, 4 (4, 5, 5, 5) sts at beg of next 2 (2, 4, 4, 8) rows—40 sts. Leave rem 40 sts on holder for back neck.

FRONT
LEFT FRONT
With straight needles, cast on 29 (33, 37, 41, 45) sts.
ROW 1 (RS) *K2, p2; rep from * to last st, k1.
ROW 2 K1, *k2, p2; rep from * to end.
Rep last 2 rows 5 times more, then row 1 once, end with a RS row.
NEXT ROW (WS) Work in pat for 8 sts, pm, work in pat to end.
NEXT (DEC) ROW (RS) Work in pat to 2 sts before marker, k2tog, sm, work in pat to end—28 (32, 36,

40, 44) sts.
Cont in rib, keeping st before marker as knit on RS rows and purl on WS rows, rep dec row every 8th row 5 times, end with a WS row—23 (27, 31, 35, 39) sts. Work even until piece measures approx 8"/20cm. Place sts on holder, do *not* break yarn.

RIGHT FRONT
With straight needles, cast on 73 (81, 89, 97, 105) sts.
ROW 1 (RS) K1, *p2, k2; rep from * to end.
ROW 2 *P2, k2; rep from * to last st, p1.
Rep last 2 rows 5 times more, then row 1 once, end with a RS row.
NEXT ROW (WS) Work in rib for 52 (60, 68, 76, 84) sts, pm, work in rib to end.
NEXT (DEC) ROW (RS) Work in rib to marker, sm, ssk, work in rib to end—72 (80, 88, 96, 104) sts.
Cont in rib, keeping st before marker as knit on RS rows and purl on WS rows, rep dec row every 8th row 5 times, end with a WS row—67 (75, 83, 91, 99) sts. Work even until piece measures approx 8"/20cm. Break yarn.

JOIN LEFT AND RIGHT FRONTS
Return 23 (27, 31, 35, 39) sts from left front to needle, ready for a RS row.
NEXT (JOINING) ROW (RS) Work in rib for 23 (27, 31, 35, 39) sts from left front, work in rib for 67 (75, 83, 91, 99) sts from right front—90 (98, 106, 114, 122) sts.
Work even in rib until piece measures 10"/25.5cm from beg, end with a RS row.

✳PODIUM PULLOVER

NEXT ROW (WS) Work in rib to first marker, remove marker, p1, pm, work in rib to 1 st before second marker, pm, p1, remove marker, work in rib to end.
NEXT (INC) ROW (RS) Work in rib to first marker, M1, sm, work in rib to second marker, sm, M1, work in rib to end—92 (104, 116, 128, 140) sts. Rep inc row every 6th row 5 times more, incorporating inc sts into k2, p2 rib—102 (114, 126, 138, 150) sts. Remove markers and cont even in rib until piece measures 16½"/42cm from beg, end with a RS row.
NEXT ROW (WS) Work in rib for 41 (49, 53, 61, 65) sts, pm for neck zipper opening, work in rib to end.

ARMHOLE SHAPING
Work armhole shapings as given for back, AT THE SAME TIME, when armhole measures 2 (2½, 3, 3½, 4)"/5 (6.5, 7.5, 9, 10)cm, make neck zipper opening as foll:
NEXT ROW (RS) Work in pat to marker, turn. Leave rem sts on holder.

UPPER LEFT FRONT
Cont on these sts until all armhole dec's are completed—50 (48, 52, 50, 54) sts. Keeping 3 sts at armhole edge in St st, work even in pat until armhole measures 6 (6½, 7, 7½, 8)"/15 (16.5, 18, 19, 20.5)cm, end with a WS row.

NECK SHAPING
NEXT ROW (RS) Work in pat for 30 (30, 32, 32, 34) sts, turn. Leave rem 20 (18, 20, 18, 20) sts on holder for front neck.
On these 30 (30, 32, 32, 34) sts only, bind off 3 sts at beg of next WS row, 2 sts at beg of next 2 WS rows, 1 st at beg of next 3 WS rows, AT THE

SAME TIME, when armhole measures same as back to shoulder, shape shoulder as given for back.

UPPER RIGHT FRONT
Return rem sts for upper right front to needle, ready for a RS row.
Cont on these sts until all armhole dec's are completed—30 (32, 32, 34, 34) sts. Keeping 3 sts at armhole edge in St st, work even in pat until armhole measures 6 (6½, 7, 7½, 8)"/15 (16.5, 18, 19, 20.5)cm, end with a WS row.

NECK SHAPING
Bind off 3 (5, 3, 5, 3) sts at beg of next RS row, 2 sts at beg of next 2 RS rows, 1 st at beg of next 3 RS rows, AT THE SAME TIME, when armhole measures same as back to shoulder, shape shoulder as given for back.

LEFT SLEEVE
LEFT SIDE
With straight needles, cast on 17 (21, 21, 25, 25) sts.
ROW 1 (RS) *K2, p2; rep from * to last st, k1.
ROW 2 P1, *k2, p2; rep from * to end.
Cont in rib as established, inc 1 st at beg of 7th and every following 6th (6th, 6th, 6th, 4th) row 19 (21, 23, 25, 27) times, incorporating inc sts into pattern. AT THE SAME TIME, when piece measures 6"/15cm from beg, place sts on holder, do *not* break yarn.

RIGHT SIDE
With straight needles, cast on 21 (21, 25, 25, 29) sts.
ROW 1 (RS) K1, *p2, k2; rep from * to end.
ROW 2 *P2, k2; rep from * to last st, p1.

Cont in rib as est, inc 1 st at end of 7th and every following 6th (6th, 6th, 6th, 4th) row 19 (21, 23, 25, 27) times, AT THE SAME TIME, when piece measures 6"/15cm from beg, place sts on holder. Break yarn.

JOIN LEFT AND RIGHT SIDES
Return sts from left side to needle, ready for a RS row.
NEXT (JOINING) ROW (RS) Keeping continuity of side inc's, pat sts from left side, pat sts from right side. Cont in pat until all inc's are complete—78 (86, 94, 102, 110) sts. Work even in rib until piece measures 19½"/49.5cm from beg, end with a WS row.

CAP SHAPING
Bind off 5 (7, 9, 11, 13) sts at beg of next 2 rows—68 (72, 76, 80, 84) sts.
ROWS 1, 3, AND 5 (DEC) (RS) K2, ssk, work in rib to last 3 sts, k2tog, k2.
ROWS 2 AND 4 (WS) P3, work in rib to last 3 sts, p3.
ROW 6 (DEC) (WS) P2, p2tog, work in rib to last 4 sts, p2tog tbl, p2—60 (64, 68, 72, 76) sts.
Rep last 6 rows 3 (3, 4, 4, 5) times more, then first 4 rows 0 (1, 0, 1, 0) times, end with a WS row—36 sts. Bind off 2 sts at beg of next 2 rows, 4 sts at beg of next 2 rows—24 sts. Bind off rem 24 sts.

RIGHT SLEEVE
LEFT SIDE
With straight needles, cast on 21 (21, 25, 25, 29) sts.
ROW 1 (RS) K1, *p2, k2; rep from * to end.
ROW 2 *P2, k2; rep from * to last st, p1.
Cont in rib as est, inc 1 st at end of

7th and every following 6th (6th, 6th, 6th, 4th) row 19 (21, 23, 25, 27) times, AT THE SAME TIME, when piece measures 6"/15cm from beg, place sts on holder, do *not* break yarn.

RIGHT SIDE

With straight needles, cast on 17 (21, 21, 25, 25) sts.

ROW 1 (RS) *K2, p2; rep from * to last st, k1.

ROW 2 P1, *k2, p2; rep from * to end.

Cont in rib as est, inc 1 st at beg of 7th and every following 6th (6th, 6th, 6th, 4th) row 19 (21, 23, 25, 27) times, AT THE SAME TIME, when piece measures 6"/15cm from beg, place sts on holder. Break yarn.

JOIN LEFT AND RIGHT SIDES

Return sts from left side to needle, ready for a RS row.

NEXT (JOINING) ROW (RS) Keeping continuity of side inc's, work in pat sts from left side and from right side. Cont in pat until all inc's are complete—78 (86, 94, 102, 110) sts. Work even in rib until piece measures 19½"/49.5cm from beg, end with a WS row.

CAP SHAPING

Bind off 5 (7, 9, 11, 13) sts at beg of next 2 rows—68 (72, 76, 80, 84) sts.

ROWS 1, 3, AND 5 (DEC) (RS) K2, ssk, work in rib to last 3 sts, k2tog, k2.

ROWS 2 AND 4 (WS) P3, work in rib to last 3 sts, p3.

ROW 6 (DEC) (WS) P2, p2tog, work in rib to last 4 sts, p2tog tbl, p2—60 (64, 68, 72, 76) sts.

Rep last 6 rows 3 (3, 4, 4, 5) times more, then first 4 rows 0 (1, 0, 1, 0) times, end with a WS row—36 sts.

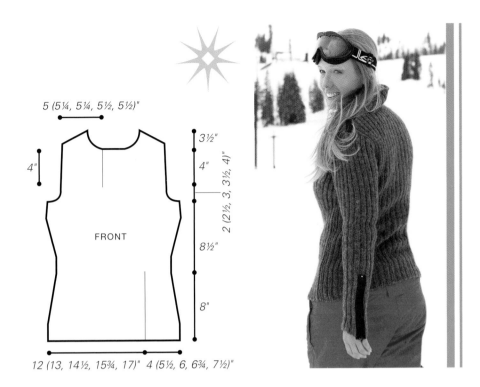

FRONT

5 (5¼, 5¼, 5½, 5½)"

4"

3½"

4"

2 (2½, 3, 3½, 4)"

8½"

8"

12 (13, 14½, 15¾, 17)"   4 (5½, 6, 6¾, 7½)"

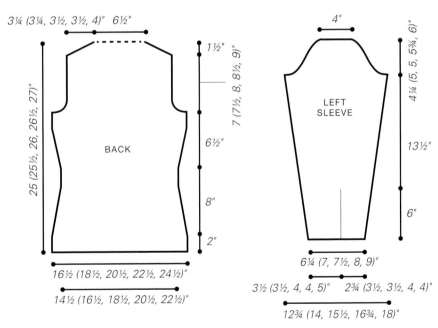

3¼ (3¼, 3½, 3½, 4)"   6½"

1½"

7 (7½, 8, 8½, 9)"

25 (25½, 26, 26½, 27)"

BACK

6½"

8"

2"

16½ (18½, 20½, 22½, 24½)"

14½ (16½, 18½, 20½, 22½)"

4"

4¼ (5, 5, 5¾, 6)"

LEFT
SLEEVE

13½"

6"

6¼ (7, 7½, 8, 9)"

3½ (3½, 4, 4, 5)"   2¾ (3½, 3½, 4, 4)"

12¾ (14, 15½, 16¾, 18)"

❋PODIUM PULLOVER

Bind off 2 sts at beg of next 2 rows, 4 sts at beg of foll 2 rows—24 sts. Bind off rem 24 sts.

FINISHING
Block pieces to finished measurements. Sew shoulder seams.

COLLAR
With circular needle and RS facing, starting at right front neck opening, pick up and k 22 sts along right front neck edge to shoulder, work in rib across 40 sts on back neck holder, pick up and k 22 (24, 22, 24, 22) sts along left front neck edge, work in rib across 20 (18, 20, 18, 20) sts on front neck holder—104 sts.
NEXT ROW (WS) P1, *k2, p2; rep from * to last 3 sts, k2, p1.
Cont in rib as est until collar measures 3¾"/9.5cm. Bind off in rib.

ZIPPERS
SHOULDER ZIPPER Fold the top edges of one 9"/23cm zipper to WS and tack in place. Line up zipper so top zipper is at bound-off edge of collar, side edge of zipper tape just covers left shoulder seam, and remainder of zipper "sits" toward left front. Trim end of zipper 1"/2.5cm longer than length of shoulder seam, being careful not to stretch seam. Stitch sides and top edge of zipper in position, either by machine or by hand. Fold extra length at armhole edge under garment and slip stitch in place from WS.
NECK ZIPPER Fold top and bottom edges of one 9"/23cm zipper to WS and tack in place. Line up zipper so top is at bound-off edge of collar, and lower edge is at start of neck opening, centering zipper teeth over opening. Stitch sides, top, and bottom edges of zipper in position.
LOWER FRONT ZIPPER With rem 9"/23 cm zipper, work as given for neck zipper, placing top at cast-on edge of front opening.
SLEEVE ZIPPER With one 7"/18cm zipper, work as given for neck zipper, placing top of zipper at cast-on edge of sleeve opening. Repeat for rem zipper/sleeve.
Set in sleeves, using sewing thread at top of sleeve cap to secure sleeve to zipper/shoulder edge. Sew side and sleeve seams. ❋

KIKKAN RANDALL
With seventeen U.S. titles and five World Cup wins so far, Kikkan needs something to keep her warm on the podium, and this cozy sweater is perfect.

Some nicknames just fit. Take "Kikkanimal," the kickingest Nordic racer the U.S. has ever known. Her list of firsts for U.S. women—World Cup podium and victory, World Championships individual medal and team gold, Olympic top ten, World Cup overall sprint champion—is especially impressive given how much runway still lies ahead. As Kikkan says, "Cross country skiers are like fine wine—we just get better with age!" She made her mark as a sprinter, but Kikkan now has medals in 5K and 10K as well. As a state champ high school runner in Alaska, Kikkan started Nordic skiing to train in the off-season. She made the Olympic team in 2002, in her birthplace of Salt Lake City, and is eyeing her fourth Olympics. At home, Kikkan trains and studies at Alaska Pacific University and is an ambassador for Fast and Female, an empowerment program for young girls.

DESIGNED BY SUZY ALLEN

CABLED CONVERTIBLE MITTENS

A winter staple, comfy cabled mittens knit in a soft neutral, become a must-have when they convert to fingerless mitts.

❋ Inspired by X Games freestyle skier TUCKER PERKINS

SIZE
Instructions are written for size Small/Medium. Instructions for Large and X-Large are in parentheses. (Shown in size Large.)

KNITTED MEASUREMENTS
• *Hand circumference*
  Approx 7 (8, 9)"/18 (20.5, 23)cm

• *Length*
  9¾ (11, 11)"/25 (28, 28)cm

MATERIALS
2 7oz/198g skeins (each approx 370yd/338m) of Red Heart *With Love* (acrylic) in #1401 pewter (4)

One set (5) size 7 (4.5mm) double-pointed needles (dpns) *or size to obtain gauge*

Cable needle (cn)

Stitch markers

Tapestry needle

GAUGE
16 sts and 25 rnds = 4"/10cm over St st using size 7 (4.5mm) needles. *Take time to check gauge.*

NOTE
Mittens are worked in 2 pieces, then seamed along back of hand.

STITCH GLOSSARY
6-ST RC Sl 4 sts to cn and hold to *back*, k2; p2, k2 from cn.
KFB Knit into front and back of next st—1 st increased.

K2, P2 RIB
(multiple of 4 sts)
RND 1 [K2, p2] to end of rnd.
Rep rnd 1 for k2, p2 rib.

CABLE PATTERN
(over 22 sts)
RNDS 1–4 P1, k1, p4, (k2, p2) 3 times, p2, k1, p1.

✻CABLED CONVERTIBLE MITTENS

RND 5 P1, k1, p4, k2, p2, 6-st RC, p4, k1, p1.
RNDS 6–10 P1, k1, p4, [k2, p2] 3 times, p2, k1, p1.
RND 11 P1, k1, p4, 6-st RC, p2, k2, p4, k1, p1.
RND 12 P1, k1, p4, [k2, p2] 3 times, p2, k1, p1.
Rep rnds 1–12 for cable pat.

RIGHT MITTEN
CUFF
Cast on 36 (40, 44) sts and divide evenly over 4 dpns.
Join to work in the rnd, taking care not to twist sts, place marker (pm) for beg of rnd.
Work in k2, p2 rib for 2½ (3, 3)"/6.5 (7.5, 7.5)cm.

BEG CABLE PAT
NEXT RND K14 (18, 22) for palm, pm, work rnd 3 (1, 1) of cable pat over next 22 sts for back of hand. Cont in St st and cable pat for 2 more rnds.*

BEG THUMB GUSSET
NEXT (INC) RND Kfb, pm for gusset, k to next marker, slip marker (sm), work next rnd of cable pat to end—2 gusset sts.
NEXT RND Work even in St st and cable pat.
NEXT (INC) RND [Kfb] twice, sm, k to next marker, sm, work in cable pat to end—4 gusset sts.
NEXT RND Work even in St st and cable pat.

NEXT (INC) RND Kfb, k to 1 st before gusset marker, kfb, sm, k to next marker, sm, work in cable pat to end—6 gusset sts.
Cont in St st and cable pat, rep last 2 rnds 1 (2, 2) times more—8 (10, 10) gusset sts. Sl gusset sts to holder to be worked later. Remove gusset marker.
NEXT (INC) RND Cast on 1 st, k to next marker, sm, work in cable pat to end—36 (40, 44) sts. Work even until rnd 11 (12, 12) of cable pat has been worked twice.
Work all sts in k2, p2 rib for 3 rnds. Bind off.

THUMB
Sl 8 (10, 10) thumb sts from holder to 2 dpns, join yarn; with third dpn, pick up and k 6 sts along thumb opening on hand—14 (16, 16) sts.
Pm, join and work in rnds of St st until thumb measures 2¾ (3, 3)"/7 (7.5, 7.5)cm from beg.
NEXT RND K2tog to end of rnd—7 (8, 8) sts. Break yarn.
Thread tail through rem sts, pull tightly to close top of thumb.

LEFT MITTEN
Cast on and work to * as for right mitten.

BEG THUMB GUSSET
NEXT (INC) RND K to marker, sm, kfb, pm for gusset, work in cable pat to end—2 gusset sts.
NEXT RND Work even.
NEXT RND K to marker, sm, [kfb] twice, sm, work in cable pat to end—4 gusset sts.
NEXT RND Work even.
NEXT RND K to marker, sm, kfb, k to 1 st before gusset marker, kfb, sm, work in cable pat to end—6 gusset

sts. Cont in St st and cable pat, rep last 2 rnds 1 (2, 2) times more—8 (10, 10) gusset sts. Sl gusset sts to holder to be worked later. Remove gusset marker.
NEXT (INC) RND K to marker, cast on 1 st, sm, work in cable pat to end—36 (40, 44) sts. Complete as for right mitten.

MITTEN TOP (MAKE 2)
Cast on 36 (40, 44) sts.
Divide evenly over 4 dpns.
Join to work in the rnd, taking care not to twist sts, pm for beg of rnd.

BEG CABLE PAT
NEXT RND Work k2, p2 rib over 14 (18, 22) sts for palm, pm, work rnd 3 (1, 1) of cable pat over next 22 sts for back of hand. Work even in k2, p2 rib and cable pat for 2 rnds more.
NEXT RND K to marker, sm, work in cable pat to end. Work even in St st and cable pat until rnd 6 of cable pat has been worked twice.

✳CABLED CONVERTIBLE MITTENS

BEG SHAPING

DEC RND 1 K2tog, k to 2 sts before marker, k2tog, sm, work in cable pat to end—12 (16, 20) palm sts.

DEC RND 2 K to marker, sm, p1, k1, p2tog, work in cable pat to last 4 sts, p2tog, k1, p1—20 cable pat sts.

Rep last 2 rnds 2 times more—8 (12, 16) palm sts, 16 cable pat sts.

DEC RND 7 K2tog, k to 2 sts before marker, k2tog, sm, work in cable pat to end—6 (10, 14) palm sts.

DEC RND 8 K to marker, sm, p1, k1, p1, k2tog, work in cable pat to last 5 sts, k2tog, p1, k1, p1—14 cable pat sts.

Rep dec rnd 7 once more—4 (8, 12) palm sts, 14 cable pat sts.

NEXT (DEC) RND K2tog to end of rnd—9 (11, 13) sts. Break yarn, leaving 10"/25.5cm tail. Thread tail through rem sts, pull tightly to secure.

FINISHING

With RS of mitten and top facing, place cast-on edge of mitten top along first k2, p2 row of mitten, matching cables. Ribbed sections of top should overlap ribbed section of mitten. Sew cabled back of mitten and top of mitten tog from WS, leaving palm sts unsewn.✳

TUCKER PERKINS
Tucker's mittens have a cool pattern that reminds him of his ski moves, and his surf moves, and whatever rad moves he happens to be doing at the moment.

Raised on New Hampshire's seacoast and surfing by age six, Tucker Perkins didn't take long to find his calling. On weekends at the family condo at Attitash, his cousins schooled him in backyard hucking off homemade jumps. He moved from racing to moguls to freeskiing, and at age fourteen his smooth style was featured in *Sports Illustrated*'s "Next Snow Search." He competed in his first X Games at seventeen, became national halfpipe champ at nineteen, and was named to the inaugural U.S. Freeskiing Team. Hard-working Tucker has enlisted Olympic aerial skier Britt Swartley and an NFL strength coach to help in his pursuit of excellence. When he's not training in Park City or competing globally, Tucker surfs, plays the drums and saxophone, works on motorcycles and cars, hunts, fishes, and dreams of meeting Bear Grylls.

DESIGNED BY TERRY KING

SNOWFLAKE HAT

This double-knit 100 percent wool hat adorned with a graphic snowflake will keep you warm and dry all day.

 Inspired by pioneer big-mountain snowboarder JEREMY JONES

SIZE
Instructions are written for size Medium.

KNITTED MEASUREMENTS
- *Brim circumference*
  18½"/47cm

- *Length*
  9½"/24cm

MATERIALS
2 1¾oz/50g balls (each approx 174yd/160m) of Rowan *Pure Wool 4 Ply* (superwash wool) in #421 glade (MC) ⬤❶

1 ball in #412 snow (CC)

Sizes 2 and 3 (2.75 and 3.25mm) circular needles, 16"/40cm long, *or size to obtain gauge*

One size 3 (3.25mm) double-pointed needle (dpn) for cast-on and bind-off

Cable needle (cn)

Stitch markers

GAUGE
24 sts and 36 rnds = 4"/10cm over St st using size 3 (3.25mm) needles. *Take time to check gauge.*

NOTES
1) One "block" on the chart represents two stitches, one knit and one purl.

2) As you are working in the round, side 1 is always facing and charts are read from right to left.
3) "POW" will be backward on side 2 of hat.

DEC (IN PAIRS)
Slip first st of 1st pair from LH needle to RH needle, slip second st of 1st

❄ SNOWFLAKE HAT

pair onto cn and hold to back, slip
first st of next pair to RH needle,
return second st of 1st pair to LH
needle, then return both first sts of
pairs to LH needle.

HAT
Working with 2 balls of MC and with
tips of both larger circular needle and
dpn held together, *cast on 1 st with
first ball of MC onto first needle,
cast on 1 st with second ball of MC
onto second needle; rep from * until
a total of 116 pairs (232 sts total)
have been cast on. Change to
smaller circular needle.

RND 1 *Bring both strands of yarn to
back of work, k1 from front needle
with first ball of MC, bring both yarns
to front of work and p1 tbl from back
needle with second ball of MC; rep
from * until 58 pairs of sts have been
worked, place marker (pm), rep from
* to end of rnd, pm for beg of rnd.

NOTE All sts are now on one circular
needle. Join and continue in the rnd.

RNDS 2–5 Work as given for rnd 1,
slipping markers each rnd. Break
second ball of MC and join CC.

RNDS 6–8 *Bring both strands of
yarn to back of work, k1 from front
needle with MC, bring both yarns to
front of work and p1 tbl from back
needle with CC; rep from * to end of
rnd, slipping markers.

BEG CHART 1
RND 9 Work 7 pairs of sts, work rnd
1 of chart 1 over next 15 sts, work
pairs of sts to end of rnd.
Work as est to end of chart 1 (rnd 6).
Rep rnd 6 until piece measures
3"/7.5cm from beg.

RNDS 15–16 *Bring both strands of
yarn to back of work, k1 from front
needle with CC, bring both yarns to
front of work and p1 tbl from back
needle with MC; rep from * to end of

CHART 1

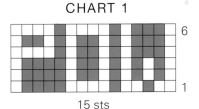

15 sts

CHART 2

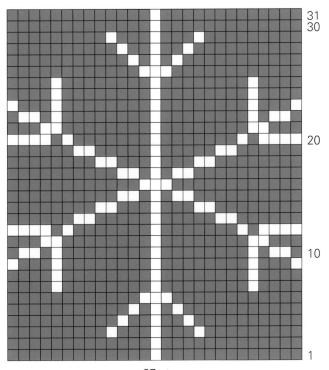

27 sts

COLOR AND STITCH KEY

■ K 1st st with MC, p tbl 2nd st with CC
□ K 1st st with CC, p tbl 2nd st with MC

❄ SNOWFLAKE HAT

rnd, slipping markers.

RND 17 *Bring both strands of yarn to back of work, k1 from front needle with MC, bring both yarns to front of work and p1 tbl from back needle with CC; rep from * to end of rnd, slipping markers.

Rep rnd 17 until piece measures 5"/12.5cm from beg.

BEG CHART 2
NEXT RND Work 15 pairs of sts, work rnd 1 of chart 2 over next 27 pairs of sts, work 31 pairs of sts, work rnd 1 of chart 2 over next 27 sts, work pairs of sts to end of rnd. Work as est to end of row 18 of chart.

TOP SHAPING
NEXT (DEC) RND *Ssk with first 2 MC sts, p2tog with first 2 CC sts, pat to 2 pairs before side marker, k2tog with next 2 MC sts, p2tog tbl with

next 2 CC sts, sl marker, repeat from * to end—54 pairs of sts.

Cont working appropriate row of chart 2 to end of chart, AT THE SAME TIME, work dec rnd every 3 rnds 4 times more—38 pairs of sts. Rep rnd 17 7 times, working dec rnd every 3 rnds—30 pairs of sts.

NEXT RND Using dpn and larger circular needle, separate inner layer from outer layer by slipping all MC sts onto dpn and all CC sts onto circular needle. When all of the sts have been separated, "tuck" needle holding CC sts inside hat, fold top of MC layer in half at markers and graft MC sts tog. Turn work inside out, fold top of CC layer in half at markers, and graft CC sts tog.

FINISHING
Block lightly to measurements. ❄

JEREMY JONES
Jeremy's hat is an homage to "Moriarty" ski hats, and also celebrates Protect Our Winters (POW), his nonprofit organization dedicated to reversing global warming. "We can't sit back and not do something. We owe that to future generations."

Snowboarding pioneer and nine-time Big Mountain Rider of the Year, Jeremy Jones started his career on a hill in his backyard and moved on to the East Coast racing circuit. But a trip to Jackson Hole convinced Jeremy to go big. His powerful heli-accessed descents on Alaska's steepest terrain have been featured in films for two decades. In 2009 he founded Jones Snowboards, which caters to big-mountain and backcountry riders. He also vowed to forego helicopters, opting instead for self-powered ascents. Jeremy lives in Truckee, California, and rides at Squaw Valley with his wife and daughter. He is working on the final installment of the *Deeper, Further, Higher* documentary trilogy.

DESIGNED BY KRISTEN ASHBAUGH-HELMREICH

DIAMOND COWL

Garter stitch diamonds bordered by twisted stitches add texture to a long cowl knit in two cozy mohair blends.

Inspired by medal-winning freestyle skier INGRID BACKSTROM

MEASUREMENTS

- *Circumference*
  56"/142cm

- *Width*
  9"/23cm

MATERIALS

2 .88oz/25g balls (each approx 229yd/210m) of Rowan *Kidsilk Haze* (mohair/silk) in #664 steel (A)

3 3½oz/100g skeins (each approx 126yd/115m) of Rowan *Cocoon* (merino/mohair) in #802 alpine (B)

Size 10½ (6.5mm) circular needle, 32"/81cm long, *or size to obtain gauge*

Cable needle (cn)

Stitch marker

GAUGE

12 sts and 24 rnds = 4"/10cm over garter st using size 10½/(6.5mm) needle and 1 strand each of A and B held together. *Take time to check gauge.*

STITCH GLOSSARY
2-ST LC Sl 1 st to cn and hold to *front*, k1; k1 from cn.
2-ST RC Sl 1 st to cn and hold to *back*, k1; k1 from cn.

COWL
With 1 strand each of A and B held tog, cast on 180 sts. Join to work in the rnd, being careful not to twist sts, place marker for beg of rnd.

Work in garter stitch (knit 1 rnd, purl 1 rnd) for 6 rounds.

BEG DIAMOND PAT
RND 1 K5, p10, *k10, p10; rep from *, end last rep k5.
RND 2 *[2-st LC, k2] twice, k4, [k2, 2-st RC] twice; rep from * to end of rnd.
RND 3 P1, *k5, p8, k5, p2; rep from *, end last rep p1.

❋DIAMOND COWL

RND 4 K1, *[2-st LC, k2] twice, k4, [2-st RC, k2] twice; rep from *, end last rep k1.

RND 5 P2, *k5, p6, k5, p4; rep from *, end last rep p2.

RND 6 K2, *[2-st LC, k2] twice, k2, [2-st RC, k2] twice, k2; rep from *, end last rep k2.

RND 7 P3, *k5, p4, k5, p6; rep from *, end last rep p3.

RND 8 K3, *[2-st LC, k2] twice, [2-st RC, k2] twice, k4; rep from *, end last rep k3.

RND 9 P4, *k5, p2, k5, p8; rep from *, end last rep p4.

RND 10 K4, *2-st LC, k2, 2-st LC, 2-st RC, k2, 2-st RC, k8; rep from *, end last rep k4.

RND 11 P5, k10, *p10, k10; rep from *, end last rep p5.

RND 12 K4, *2-st RC, k2, 2-st RC, 2-st LC, k2, 2st LC, k8; rep from *, end last rep k4.

RND 13 P4, *k5, p2, k5, p8; rep from *, end last rep p4.

RND 14 K3, *[2-st RC, k2] twice, [2-st LC, k2] twice, k4; rep from *, end last rep k3.

RND 15 P3, *k5, p4, k5, p6; rep from *, end last rep p3.

RND 16 K2, *[2-st RC, k2] twice, k2, [2-st LC, k2] twice, k2; rep from *, end last rep k2.

RND 17 P2, *k5, p6, k5, p4; rep from *, end last rep p2.

RND 18 K1, *[2-st RC, k2] twice, k4, [2-st LC, k2] twice; rep from *, end last rep k1.

RND 19 P1, *k5, p8, k5, p2; rep from *, end last rep p1.

RND 20 *[2-st RC, k2] twice, k4, [k2, 2-st LC] twice; rep from * to end of rnd.
Rep rnds 1–20 once more.
Beg with a purl rnd, work in garter stitch for 6 rnds. Bind off knitwise.

FINISHING
Block lightly to measurements.❋

INGRID BACKSTROM

Ingrid loves a good loop cowl. "I think a really soft knitted one could be cool." So here you go, Ingrid. This one's for you, and everyone who wants to be just like you!

She has been called "the Goddess of Gnar," and for good reason. Ingrid Backstrom is a regular on the podium at big-mountain freeskiing contests. Also, *Powder* magazine has honored her with five Female Performance of the Year awards for her epic descents, from China to Baffin Island to Denali. The Seattle-ite grew up taking on the slopes of Crystal Mountain in a "brat pack" with her brother, Arne, while her parents were ski patrolling. She quickly learned to appreciate independence and freedom. After taking a year off to ski bum in Squaw Valley, Tahoe, she entered her first freeskiing contest in nearby Kirkwood. After placing third, she was hooked. She has appeared in thirteen ski films, won seventeen awards, and logged a whole lot of miles. Her advice to those who want to follow in her tracks is to "ski because you love it."

DESIGNED BY SUZY ALLEN

SKI PATROL HOODIE & MITTENS

Your little ski bum will be ready for patrol this winter in an adorable sweater and mitten set.

 Inspired by future Olympic champion HUCK ZANDER

SIZES

SWEATER
Child's 4 (6, 8, 10)

MITTENS
Child's 4 (6, 8/10)

KNITTED MEASUREMENTS

SWEATER:
- *Chest*
  32 (34, 35½, 37)"/81 (86.5, 90, 94)cm

- *Length*
  15 (17½, 19½, 20)"/38 (44.5, 49.5, 51)cm

- *Upper arm*
  11 (12, 13½, 13½)"/28 (30.5, 34.5, 34.5)cm

MITTEN
- *Hand circumference*
  5½ (6½, 7½)"/14 (16.5, 19)cm

- *Length from cuff to fingertip*
  6 (6½, 7)"/15 (16.5, 18)cm

MATERIALS

4 (5, 6, 6) 7oz/198g skeins (each approx 370yd/338m) of Red Heart *With Love* (acrylic) in #1909 holly berry (MC) 🔳4🔳

1 skein in #1101 eggshell (CC)

One pair size 7 (4.5mm) needles *or size to obtain gauge*

One set (5) each sizes 6 and 8 (4 and 5mm) double-pointed needles (dpns) (for mittens)

Stitch holder or waste yarn

1 separating zipper

GAUGE

18 sts and 24 rows = 4"/10 cm over St st using size 7 (4.5mm) needles. *Take time to check gauge.*

✳SKI PATROL HOODIE & MITTENS

K2, P2 RIB
(multiple of 4 sts)
ROW/RND 1 (RS) *K2, p2;
rep from * to end.
Rep row/rnd 1 for k2, p2 rib.

NOTE
Charts may also be worked in
duplicate st upon completion of
garment or mittens.

BACK
With MC, cast on 72 (76, 80, 84) sts.
Work in k2, p2 rib for 2"/5cm, end
with a WS row.
Starting with a knit (RS) row,
work in St st (k on RS, p on WS) until
piece measures 9 (11, 12½,
13)"/23(28, 32, 33)cm from beg,
end with a WS row.

ARMHOLE SHAPING
Bind off 3 sts at beg of next 2 rows,
2 sts at beg of foll 2 rows. Dec 1 st
at each end of next row—60 (64, 68,
72) sts. Work even until armhole
measures 5 (5½, 6, 6½)"/12.5 (14,
15, 16.5)cm, end with a WS row.

NECK SHAPING
NEXT ROW (RS) K24 (25, 26, 28),
join a 2nd ball of yarn and
bind off center 12 (14, 16, 16) sts,
knit to end.
Working both sides at same time,
bind off 3 sts from each neck edge
once—21 (22, 23, 25) sts rem each
side for shoulder. Work even until
armhole measures 6 (6½, 7, 7)"/15
(16.5, 18, 18)cm, end with a WS row.
Bind off rem sts each side for
shoulder.

RIGHT FRONT
With MC, cast on 37 (39, 41, 43) sts.
ROW 1 (RS) K3, *p2, k2; rep from *
to last 2 (0, 2, 0) sts, p2 (0, 2, 0).
ROW 2 K2 (0, 2, 0), *p2, k2; rep from

* to last 3 sts, p3.
Cont in k2, p2 rib as est for 2"/5cm,
end with a WS row.
NEXT ROW (RS) K3, p1, knit to end.
NEXT ROW Purl to last 4 sts, k1, p3.
Cont as est until piece measures 9
(11, 12½, 13)"/23 (28, 32, 33)cm
from beg, end with a RS row.

ARMHOLE SHAPING
Bind off 3 sts at beg of next WS row,
2 sts at beg of foll WS row.
Dec 1 st at end of next RS row—31
(33, 35, 37) sts. Work 1 row even,
end with a WS row.

BEG CHART 1
NEXT ROW (RS) K3, p1, k1, work
row 1 of chart 1 over next 20 sts,
knit to end.
NEXT ROW P6 (8, 10, 12),
work row 2 of chart 1 over next 20
sts, p1, k1, p3.
Cont as est to end of chart.
NEXT ROW (RS) K3, p1, knit to end.
NEXT ROW Purl to last 4 sts, k1, p3.
Work even in pat until armhole
measures 4½ (4½, 5, 5"/11.5 (11.5,
12.5, 12.5)cm, end with a WS row.

NECK SHAPING
Bind off 4 sts at beg of next RS row,
3 sts at beg of foll RS row, 2 sts at
beg of foll RS row. Dec 1 st at beg of
every RS row 1 (2, 3, 3) times—21
(22, 23, 25) sts. Work even until
armhole measures same as back to
shoulder, end with a WS row.
Bind off rem sts.

LEFT FRONT
With MC, cast on 37 (39, 41, 43) sts.
ROW 1 (RS) P2 (0, 2, 0), *k2, p2; rep
from * to last 3 sts, k3.
ROW 2 P3, *k2, p2; rep from * to last
2 sts, k2 (0, 2, 0).
Cont in k2, p2 rib as est for 2"/5cm,
end with a WS row.

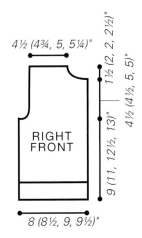

4½ (4¾, 5, 5¼)"

RIGHT FRONT

1½ (2, 2, 2½)"
4½ (4½, 5, 5)"
9 (11, 12½, 13)"

8 (8½, 9, 9½)"

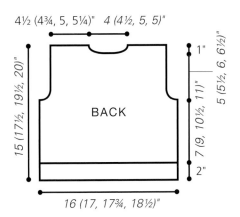

4½ (4¾, 5, 5¼)"   4 (4½, 5, 5)"

BACK

15 (17½, 19½, 20)"
5 (5½, 6, 6½)"
1"
7 (9, 10½, 11)"
2"

16 (17, 17¾, 18½)"

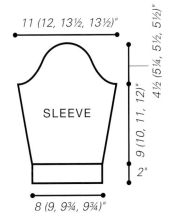

11 (12, 13½, 13½)"

SLEEVE

4½ (5¼, 5½, 5½)"
9 (10, 11, 12)"
2"

8 (9, 9¾, 9¾)"

✳SKI PATROL HOODIE & MITTENS

CHART 1

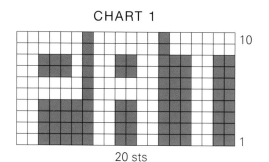

20 sts

CHART 2

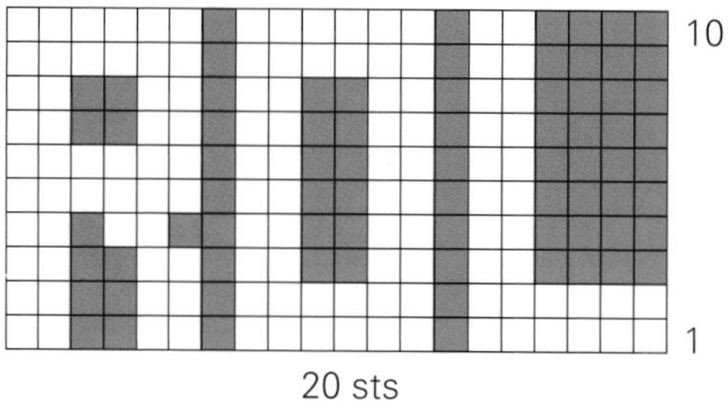

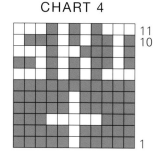

20 sts

CHART 3

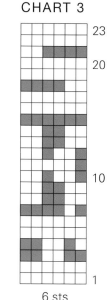

6 sts

COLOR KEY

■ Holly berry (MC)
□ Eggshell (CC)

CHART 4

11 sts

NEXT ROW (RS) Knit to last 4 sts, p1, k3.
NEXT ROW P3, k1, purl to end.
Cont as est until piece measures 9 (11, 12½, 13)"/23 (28, 32, 33)cm from beg, end with a WS row.

ARMHOLE SHAPING

Bind off 3 sts at beg of next RS row, 2 sts at beg of foll RS row.
Dec 1 st at beg of next RS row—31 (33, 35, 37) sts. Work 1 row even, end with a WS row.

BEG CHART 2

NEXT ROW (RS) K6 (8, 10, 12), work row 1 of chart 2 over next 20 sts, k1, p1, k3.
NEXT ROW P3, k1, p1, work row 2 of chart 2 over next 20 sts, purl to end of row.
Cont as est to end of chart.
NEXT ROW (RS) Knit to last 4 sts, p1, k3.
NEXT ROW P3, k1, purl to end.
Work even in pat until armhole measures 4½ (4½, 5, 5)"/11.5 (11.5, 12.5, 12.5)cm, end with a RS row.

NECK SHAPING

Bind off 4 sts at beg of next WS row, 3 sts at beg of foll WS row, 2 sts at beg of foll WS row. Dec 1 st at beg of every RS row 1 (2, 3, 3) times—

21 (22, 23, 25) sts. Work even until armhole measures same as back to shoulder, end with a WS row.
Bind off rem sts.

LEFT SLEEVE

With MC, cast on 36 (40, 44, 44) sts.
Work in k2, p2 rib for 2"/5cm, end with a WS row.
Starting with a knit (RS) row, work in St st, inc 1 st at each end of 7th and every foll 6th row 6 (6, 7, 7) times—50 (54, 60, 60) sts. Work even until piece measures 11 (12, 13, 14)"/28 (30.5, 33, 35.5)cm, end with a WS row.

CAP SHAPING

Bind off 3 sts at beg of next 2 rows, 2 sts at beg of foll 2 (2, 4, 4) rows.
Dec 1 st at each end of next and every RS row 10 (12, 12, 12) times—18 (18, 20, 20) sts. Bind off 3 sts at beg of next 2 rows. Bind off rem 12 (12, 14, 14) sts.

RIGHT SLEEVE

Work as given for left sleeve, AT THE SAME TIME, when piece measures 6½"/16.5cm from beg, work chart 3 over center 6 sts.

FINISHING

Block pieces lightly to measurements. Sew shoulder seams.

HOOD

With MC and RS facing, pick up and k 51 (55, 60, 64) sts evenly around neck opening.
ROWS 1 AND 3 (WS) K3, purl to last 3 sts, k3.
ROW 2 K3, *M1, k2; rep from * to last 4 (4, 3, 3) sts, M1, k4 (4, 3, 3)—74 (80, 88, 94) sts.
ROW 4 Knit.
Rep rows 3 and 4 until hood measures 8 (9, 10, 10½)"/20.5 (23, 25.5, 26.6)cm from pick-up row, end with a WS row. Bind off.

✳SKI PATROL HOODIE & MITTENS

Fold bound-off edge of hood in half and sew top seam. Set in sleeves. Sew side and sleeve seams. Sew zipper to center front edges.

CROSS APPLIQUÉ
With CC, cast on 15 sts. Work 20 rows in garter st (knit every row). Cast on 14 sts at beg of next 2 rows—43 sts.
Work a further 18 rows in garter st. Bind off 14 sts at beg of next 2 rows—15 sts.
Work a further 23 sts in garter st, end with a RS row. Bind off all sts knitwise.
Sew cross appliqué to back, placing cast-on edge approx 3½"/9cm from lower edge and centering cross.

MITTEN (MAKE 2)
With smaller dpns and MC, cast on 24 (28, 32) sts, distributing evenly over 4 needles. Join to work in the rnd, being careful not to twist sts, and place marker (pm) for beg of rnd. Work in rnds of k2, p2 rib for 2"/5cm.
NEXT RND With MC, knit, inc 2 sts evenly around—26 (30, 34) sts. Change to larger dpns and knit a further 2 rnds.

THUMB GUSSET
RND 1 Kfb, pm, knit to end.
RND 2 Kfb, knit to last st before marker, kfb, slip marker (sm), knit to end.
Rep last rnd 3 (4, 4) times more—10 (12, 12) sts between markers.

HAND
NEXT RND Place first 10 (12, 12) sts on holder (or waste yarn), cast on 1 st, knit to end—26 (30, 36) sts. Work 3 (4, 5) rnds even in St st.

BEG CHART 4
NEXT RND K1 (2, 3), work row 1 of chart 4 over next 11 sts, k2 (4, 7), work row 1 of chart 4 over next 11 sts, k1 (2, 4).
Cont as est to end of chart. Work even in St st until mitten measures 5 (5½, 6)"/12.5 (14, 15)cm from beg.

TOP SHAPING
RND 1 [K2tog, k9 (11, 14), ssk] twice—22 (26, 32) sts.
RND 2 [K2tog, k7 (9, 12), ssk] twice—18 (22, 28) sts.
Cont as est, working 2 fewer sts between decs every row until 10 (10, 12) sts rem. Break yarn, leaving a long tail. Thread tail through rem sts and fasten off.

THUMB
Place 10 (12, 12) sts on holder from thumb onto smaller dpn, ready for a RS row.
RND 1 K10 (12, 12) from thumb holder, pick up and k 2 sts along cast-on edge of thumb opening, distributing sts evenly over 4 dpns—12 (14, 14) sts. Knit 8 (10, 12) rnds or desired length for thumb.
NEXT RND *K2tog; rep from * to end of rnd—5 (6, 6) sts.
Break yarn, leaving a long tail. Thread tail through rem sts and fasten off.✳

HUCK ZANDER
With a name like Huck, and a standing challenge to Tommy Moe, this budding speedster had to be dressed in a zip hoodie with ski patrol markings—so he can get on their good side from the start.

Huck Zander took his first ski run at the age of six months . . . in a baby carrier behind his parents' house in Truckee, California. A year later he moved on to greater challenges by taking on the backcountry in a backpack. Huck took to screaming "More! More! Faster! Faster!" at the bottom of every pitch, inspiring his parents to transition him to self-powered descents. At two and a half, Huck finally tried out his own skis on his home mountain at Squaw Valley. He got five days in that year, adhering to a self-designed progression of three runs on the chair lift . . . no more, no less. At the bottom of the lift he was heard telling the liftie, "The ski police will never catch me because I'm wayyyy too fast!" Huck's idol is downhill star Tommy Moe, though he is already calling Tommy out.

DESIGNED BY LORNA MISER

REVERSIBLE CABLE SCARF

A reversible cable and a variegated wool-blend yarn are
the perfect combo for color, texture, and warmth.

 Inspired by Olympic alpine skier **ALICE MCKENNIS**

KNITTED MEASUREMENTS

• *Width*
Approx 10"/25.5cm

• *Length*
Approx 51"/129.5cm

MATERIALS

2 3½oz/100g skeins
(each approx 151yd/138m) of
Red Heart *Boutique Treasure*
(acrylic/wool) in #1930
horizon (4)

One pair size 10½
(6.5mm) needles *or size to
obtain gauge*

Cable needle (cn)

Stitch markers

GAUGE

12 sts and 18 rows = 4"/10cm
over basketweave pat using size
10½ (6.5mm) needles.
Take time to check gauge.

❄ REVERSIBLE CABLE SCARF

BASKETWEAVE PATTERN
(multiple of 8 sts)
ROWS 1–4 *K4, p4;
rep from * to end.
ROWS 5–8 *P4, k4;
rep from * to end.
Rep rows 1–8 for basketweave pat.

REVERSIBLE CABLE PATTERN
(worked over 8 sts)
ROWS 1–7 [K1, p1] 4 times.
ROW 8 (RS) Sl 4 sts to cn and
hold to *front*, [k1, p1] twice, then
[k1, p1] twice from cn.

SCARF
Cast on 40 sts.
ROW 1 (RS) Work basketweave pat
over 16 sts, place marker (pm), work
reversible cable over center 8 sts,
pm, work basketweave pat over rem
16 sts. Mark this row as WS, sl
markers every row.
Work even in pats until scarf
measures approx 51"/129.5cm from
beg, or until approx 54"/137cm of
yarn rem, end with a row 4 or 7.
Bind off.

FINISHING
Block lightly to measurements. ❄

ALICE MCKENNIS
This scarf was modeled
after one Alice made on
the road racing in Europe
that doubles as a mini
blanket. "It gives me
some of that home
comfort feeling when
I'm thousands of miles
away from Colorado!"

Alice McKennis is a quick learner.
Raised on a ranch in Colorado,
Alice made her first turns at
Sunlight Mountain Resort before
the age of two, was ski racing at
age five, and by fourteen had
given up her equestrian pursuits
to race full-time. She made the
2010 Olympics in her rookie
World Cup season and, despite
breaking her leg in 2011, was
back in 2012 as part of the U.S.
women's alpine speed team that
crushed the European
competition. In 2013 she won her
first World Cup downhill in St.
Anton, Austria. Go Alice! When
not on the slopes Alice loves
riding horses and her mountain
bike, fishing, camping, and
listening to country music.

FAIR ISLE SKI HAT

With stranded colorwork, generous ribbing, and a warm wool yarn, this hat is made to weather the cold.

✳ Inspired by Olympic champion alpine skier BARBARA ANN COCHRAN

SIZE
Adult Medium

KNITTED MEASUREMENTS
• *Brim circumference*
  17½"/44.5cm

• *Length*
  9"/23cm

MATERIALS
1 1¾oz/50g ball (each approx 174yd/160m) of Rowan *Pure Wool 4 Ply* (superwash wool) each in #451 porcelaine (A), #450 eau de nil (B), and #461 ochre (C) **1**

One each sizes 2 and 3 (2.75 and 3.25mm) circular needle, 16"/40cm long, *or size to obtain gauge*

One set (5) size 3 (3.25mm) double-pointed needles (dpns)

Stitch marker

Pompom maker (optional)

GAUGE
30 sts and 36 rnds = 4"/10cm over Fair Isle pat using size 3 (3.25mm) needles.
Take time to check gauge.

K2, P2 RIB
(multiple of 4 sts)
RND 1 *K2, p2; rep from * to end of rnd.
Rep rnd 1 for k2, p2 rib.

STRIPE PATTERN
RNDS 1, 2, 6, AND 7 With A, knit.
RNDS 3–5 With C, knit.
RNDS 8–10 With B, knit.
Rep rnds 1–10 for stripe pat.

NOTE
Change to dpns when there are too few sts to fit comfortably on circular needle.

HAT
With smaller circular needle and C, cast on 132 sts. Break C and join A. Join to work in the rnd, being careful not to twist sts, and place marker (pm) for beg of rnd. Work in k2, p2

✳FAIR ISLE SKI HAT

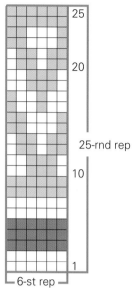

25-rnd rep

6-st rep

COLOR KEY
☐ Porcelaine (A)
◻ Eau de nil (B)
◼ Ochre (C)

BARBARA ANN COCHRAN
This hat is based on one Barbara Ann received when she gave a presentation at Colby College. "I love the design on it . . . I've always loved knit hats. Growing up, we didn't ski with helmets, so hats were what kept us warm."

rib for 1¾"/4.5cm.
Change to larger circular needle.

BEG CHART
NEXT RND Continuing in St st, work 6-st rep of chart 22 times.
Cont in pat as established, working rnds 1–25 of chart twice.

CROWN SHAPING
Working in stripe pat, shape crown as foll, using appropriate colors:
RND 1 *Ssk, k8, k2tog; rep from * to end of rnd—110 sts. Work 4 rnds even in pat.
RND 6 *Ssk, k6, k2tog; rep from * to end of rnd—88 sts. Work 4 rnds even in pat.
RND 11 *Ssk, k4, k2tog; rep from * to end of rnd—66 sts. Work 2 rnds even in pat.

RND 14 *Ssk, k2, k2tog; rep from * to end of rnd—44 sts. Work 2 rnds even in pat.
RND 17 *Ssk, k2tog; rep from * to end of rnd—22 sts. Work 2 rnds even in pat.
RND 20 *K2tog; rep from * to end of rnd—11 sts.
Break yarn, leaving a long tail. Thread tail through rem sts and pull tightly to secure.

FINISHING
Block lightly to measurements.

POMPOM
Using one strand of each yarn held together, make a loose pompom 4"/10cm in diameter. Sew to top of hat.✳

Part of the famous skiing Cochran family, Barbara Ann grew up in Richmond, Vermont, skiing day and night with her three siblings on the rope tow that her father built on the hill behind their house. Dad Mickey coached all four kids—Bobby, Marilyn, Lindy, and Barbara Ann—to the U.S. Ski Team and the Olympics, and Barbara Ann won gold in the Olympic slalom in 1972. That rope tow is now Cochran's Ski Area, the first nonprofit ski area in the country, where Barbara Ann teaches tomorrow's stars as they make their first turns—that's when she's not practicing her new vocation as a sports psychologist. Among the next generation of skiing Cochrans, six have made the U.S. Ski Team, including Barbara Ann's son, Ryan Cochran-Siegle.

DOWNHILL PULLOVER

This stunning Fair Isle sweater, knit in a warm merino-alpaca blend, features graphic snowflake and skier motifs.

❋ Inspired by Olympian and World Champion in speed skiing FRANZ WEBER

SIZES

Instructions are written for unisex size X-Small. Changes for Small, Medium, Large, X-Large, and XX-Large are in parentheses. (Shown in size Medium.)

KNITTED MEASUREMENTS

- *Chest*
  38 (42, 44, 46½, 49, 52)"/96.5 (106.5, 112, 118, 124.5, 132)cm

- *Length*
  23¼ (24½, 25, 26, 26½, 27)"/59 (62, 63.5, 66, 67.5, 68.5)cm

- *Upper arm*
  13¼ (14, 15, 15½, 16½, 17)"/33.5 (35.5, 38, 39.5, 43)cm

MATERIALS

5 (6, 7, 7, 8, 8) 1¾oz/50g balls (each approx 191yd/175m) of Rowan *Felted Tweed DK* (merino/alpaca/viscose) in #159 carbon (MC) (4)

3 (4, 4, 4, 5, 5) balls in #177 clay (CC)

One pair each sizes 3 and 5 (3.25 and 3.75mm) needles *or size to obtain gauge*

Size 3 (3.25mm) circular needle, 16"/40cm long

Stitch holders

GAUGE

25 sts and 28 rows = 4"/10cm over Fair Isle pat using size 5 (3.75mm) needles.
Take time to check gauge.

K2, P2 RIB
(multiple of 4 sts)

ROW/RND 1 (RS) *K2, p2; rep from * to end.
Rep row/rnd 1 for k2, p2 rib.

K2, P2 RIB
(multiple of 4 sts plus 2)

ROW 1 (RS) *K2, p2; rep from * to last 2 sts, k2.

❋DOWNHILL PULLOVER

ROW 2 *P2, k2; rep from * to last 2 sts, p2.
Rep rows 1 and 2 for k2, p2 rib.

NOTES

1) Charts are worked in St st (k on RS, p on WS) throughout.
2) Work charts 1 and 3 using Fair Isle stranding technique and chart 2 using intarsia technique, winding small balls of CC.
3) Shapings are *not* included in charts.

BACK

With smaller needles and MC, cast on 122 (134, 138, 146, 154, 166) sts. Work in k2, p2 rib for 3"/8cm, end with a WS row and dec 3 (3, 1, 1, 1, 3) sts evenly across last row—119 (131, 137, 145, 153, 163) sts.
Change to larger needles.

BEG CHART 1

ROW 1 (RS) Beg with row 9 (5, 5, 1, 1, 1), work sts 1–40 (35–40, 32–40, 28–40, 24–40, 19–40) of chart 1 once, work 40-st rep 1 (3, 3, 3, 3, 3) times, work sts 1–39 (1–5, 1–8, 1–12, 1–16, 1–21).
Cont to follow chart in this way through row 72, then rep rows 1–18 once, end with a WS row.

BEG CHART 2

NEXT ROW (RS) Beg with row 1, work sts 20–22 (14–22, 11–22, 7–22, 3–22, 20–22) of chart 2 once, work 22-st rep 5 (5, 5, 5, 6, 7) times, work sts 1–6 (1–12, 1–15, 1–19, 1, 1–6).

Cont to follow chart in this way through row 4, end with a WS row. Piece should measure approx 16 (16½, 16½, 17, 17, 17)"/40.5 (42, 42, 43, 43, 43)cm from beg.

ARMHOLE SHAPING

Keeping continuity of chart, bind off 8 (8, 9, 9, 10, 11) sts at beg of next 2 rows. Dec 1 st at each end of next 5 rows, every RS row 6 (7, 5, 5, 5, 3) times, then every 4th row 0 (2, 3, 3, 3, 4) times—81 (87, 93, 101, 107, 117) sts. Cont even through row 40 of chart 2, end with a WS row.

BEG CHART 3

NEXT ROW (RS) Beg with row 1, work sts 20–40 (17–40, 14–40, 10–40, 7–40, 2–40) of chart 3 once, work 40-st rep once, work sts 1–20 (1–23, 1–26, 1–30, 1–33, 1–38).
Cont to follow chart in this way until armhole measures 6¾ (7½, 8, 8½, 9, 10)"/17 (19, 20.5, 21.5, 23, 25.5)cm, end with a WS row.

NECK AND SHOULDER SHAPING

NEXT ROW (RS) Bind off 6 (7, 8, 9, 10, 11) sts, work in pat until there are 14 (18, 19, 22, 23, 26) sts on RH needle, turn. Place rem sts on holder.
NEXT ROW (WS) P2tog, work in pat to end of row.
NEXT ROW Bind off 7 (8, 8, 10, 10, 12) sts, work in pat to last 2 sts, k2tog. Work 1 row even in pat. Bind off rem 7 (8, 9, 10, 11, 12) sts.
With RS facing, rejoin yarn to sts on holder, bind off center 37 (37, 39, 39, 41, 43) sts, work in pat to end of row. Complete to match first side, reversing shapings.

FRONT

Work as given for back until armhole measures 4¼ (5, 5½, 6, 6½, 7½)"/10.5 (12.5, 14, 15, 16.5, 19)cm, end with a WS row.

NECK SHAPING

NEXT ROW (RS) Work in pat for 27 (30, 32, 36, 39, 43) sts, turn. Place rem sts on holder.
Dec 1 st at neck edge every row 4 times, then every RS row 2 (2, 2, 2, 3, 3) times, then every 4th row once—20 (23, 25, 29, 31, 35) sts. Work even until armhole measures same as back to shoulder. Shape shoulder as given for back.
With RS facing, rejoin yarn to sts on holder, bind off center 27 (27, 29, 29, 29, 31) sts, work in pat to end of row. Complete to match first side, reversing shapings.

SLEEVES

With smaller needles and MC, cast on 54 (54, 58, 58, 62, 66) sts. Work in k2, p2 rib for 3"/8cm, end with a WS row and dec 3 (1, 3, 1, 1, 3) sts evenly across last row—51 (53, 55, 57, 61, 63) sts.
Change to larger needles.

BEG CHART 1

ROW 1 (RS) Beg with row 9 (5, 5, 1, 1, 1), work sts 36–40 (35–40, 34–40, 33–40, 31–40, 30–40) of chart 1 once, work 40-st rep once, work sts 1–6 (1–7, 1–8, 1–9, 1–11, 1–12).
Cont to follow chart in this way through row 72, then rep rows 1–72, AT THE SAME TIME, inc 1 st at each end of 5th and every following 4th row 10 (8, 9, 9, 12, 14) times, then

❊DOWNHILL PULLOVER

CHART 3

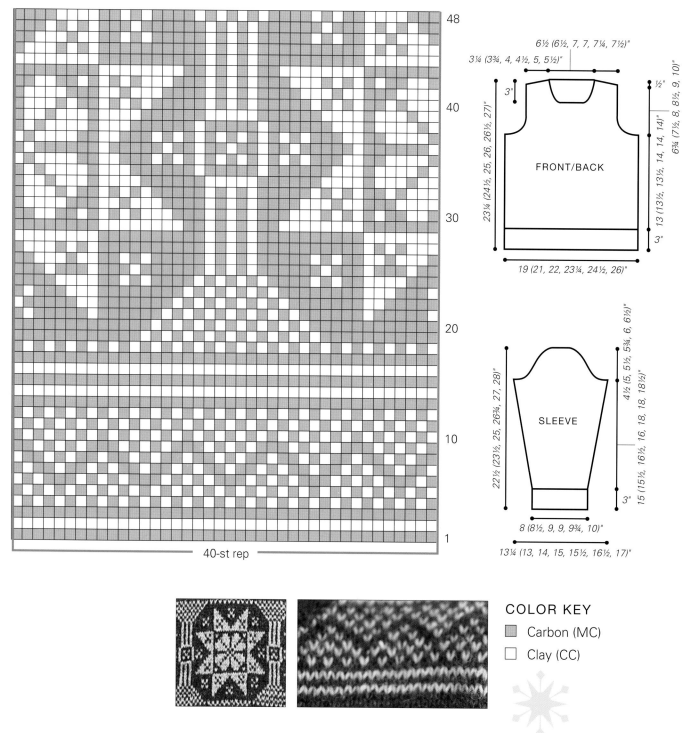

40-st rep

Front/Back measurements:
6½ (6½, 7, 7, 7¼, 7½)"
3¼ (3¾, 4, 4½, 5, 5½)"
3"
½"
23¼ (24½, 25, 26, 26½, 27)"
6¾ (7½, 8, 8½, 9, 10)"
13 (13½, 13½, 14, 14, 14)"
3"
FRONT/BACK
19 (21, 22, 23¼, 24½, 26)"

Sleeve measurements:
4½ (5, 5½, 5¾, 6, 6½)"
22½ (23½, 25, 26¾, 27, 28)"
15 (15½, 16, 16, 18, 18½)"
SLEEVE
3"
8 (8½, 9, 9, 9¾, 10)"
13¼ (13, 14, 15, 15½, 16½, 17)"

COLOR KEY
- ▨ Carbon (MC)
- ☐ Clay (CC)

CHART 1

72
70

60

50

40

72-row
rep

30

20

10

1

40-st rep

139

☀DOWNHILL PULLOVER

CHART 2

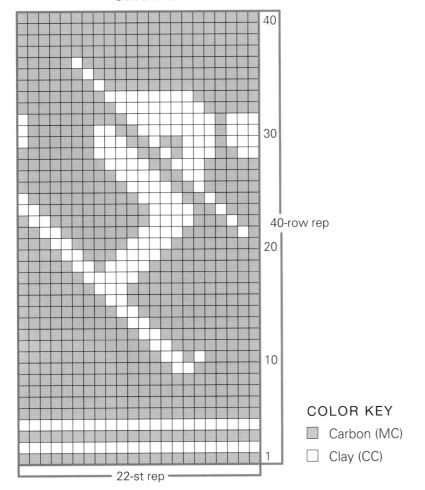

40-row rep

22-st rep

COLOR KEY

▨ Carbon (MC)

☐ Clay (CC)

every 6th row 5 (8, 9, 10, 8, 7) times—83 (87, 93, 97, 103, 107) sts. Work even in pat until piece measures 18 (18½, 19½, 21, 21, 21½)"/45.5 (47, 49.5, 53.5, 53.5, 54.5)cm from beg, end with a WS row.

CAP SHAPING

Keeping continuity of chart, bind off 8 (8, 9, 9, 10, 11) sts at beg of next 2 rows. Dec 1 st at each end of next 5 rows, every RS row once, every 4th row 1 (1, 2, 2, 2, 2) times, every RS row 8 (7, 6, 6, 6, 8) times, then every row 0 (3, 5, 7, 9, 9) times, end with a WS row—37 sts. Bind off

9 sts at beg of next 2 rows. Bind off rem 19 sts.

FINISHING

Block pieces to measurements. Sew shoulder seams.

NECKBAND

With circular needle and MC, starting and ending at left shoulder, pick up and k 104 (104, 108, 108, 116, 116) sts evenly around neck opening. Join to work in the rnd. Work in k2, p2 rib for 1¼"/3cm. Bind off in rib. Set in sleeves. Sew side and sleeve seams. Block lightly to measurements.☀

How fast is 222.222 kph? It's a shade over 138 mph, and it's how fast Franz Weber has gone on skis. A native of Igls, Austria, the 1977 European skateboard champ moved to the U.S. in 1982, settling in Reno, Nevada. He took up speed skiing on the World Pro Tour, setting three records and spending six consecutive years as World Speed Skiing Champion. He retired after the 1992 Olympics to run Franz Weber, Inc., which represents ski legends and organizes client hospitality and corporate outings, including the Tour de Franz cycling trips and Franz and Friends fantasy ski adventures. Among many honors, Franz is a recipient of the Schneekristall award, granting him lifelong free skiing privileges in Austria. *Wunderbar!* As a member of the Reno Tahoe Winter Games Coalition, he hopes to bring the Winter Olympic Games back to the Sierras.

✳ KNIT NOTES

✳ GUIDE TO FIBERS FOR COLD-WEATHER KNITTING

ACRYLIC
Strong, durable, easy to care for, and makes fabric with elasticity and memory. A good choice for people who have trouble wearing animal fibers. Alone, acrylic may not be warm enough for active sports. Innovations in the technology for making acrylic yarns mean that it can be formed in many ways. Whether used to make another fiber stronger, add sheen or texture, or keep the price affordable, acrylic-blend yarns can add to a skier's wardrobe.

ALPACA
Warmer than wool, durable, and light, alpaca yarns come from a camelid native to the Andes, where staying warm is essential to survival. When damp, alpaca keeps the wearer feeling warm. Not as much elasticity as wool. A garment in sport-weight alpaca may feel as warm as the same garment in worsted-weight wool. People who cannot wear wool may be able to wear alpaca next to the skin. Of the two grades of alpaca, suri is silkier and more rare than huacaya.

ANGORA
Angora is very warm, very soft, very light in weight for its volume. Absorbs moisture and keeps the wearer feeling warm and dry. Spun from the fur of rabbits, angora yarn has a distinctive halo of fluffy hairs, which can shed, during knitting as well as wearing. Knitted fabric made from pure angora has little elasticity; this makes it less effective for socks or mitten cuffs, where ribbing has a structural function. Angora is a luxurious addition to blends where softness and halo are desired, and pure angora is a luxurious, warming accent to a garment in another fiber.

BISON
The hardy American bison, commonly called American buffalo, has a dense coat containing different kinds of fibers. The finest, innermost layer is the down, which spins into soft, lightweight, warm, luxurious yarn. Bison yarn compares favorably to wool. Bison is better at keeping the wearer warm, even when the fiber is wet. Felted mittens and hats are very warm indeed.

CASHMERE
Very warm and soft, cashmere is lighter in weight and provides greater insulation than wool alone. The goats that provide us with cashmere fiber originally come from the Himalayas, so it is little wonder that cashmere is a nearly ideal fiber for cold weather. Cashmere is expensive on its own; it combines well with other fibers where its light weight and insulating properties are assets.

COTTON
Durable, heavy, and strong—actually stronger wet than dry—cotton has little memory and drapes beautifully. Cotton's absorbency leaves the wearer feeling cool, making it better for wear in hot weather than cold weather. For snowy weather, cotton alone works well for accessories or garments worn indoors.

LINEN
Very strong and durable, linen feels cool to the wearer. Linen becomes softer while being knitted and softer with wear and laundering. Linen fabric has no memory. For a skier, linen is a good choice for scarves or tops to wear indoors and is appreciated for its weight and drape.

MOHAIR
Warm, absorbent so that damp fabric feels warm to the wearer, and often has more sheen than wool. An inherently fluffy fiber from angora goats with various grades of fineness in yarns, kid mohair is the rarest, softest, and easiest type for many people to wear next to the skin. If the fuzziness of mohair feels scratchy, put another layer between the skin and mohair. Mohair is often combined with other fibers in blends where its halo is an asset.

QIVIUT
The epitome of fibers for cold, snowy climates. Spun from the fine undercoat of the musk ox, a native of the Arctic. Extremely warm, soft, and lightweight. Also rare and expensive, so qiviut is usually reserved for cowls and other small accessories.

SILK
Long considered a luxurious fiber, silk is warm, strong, and lustrous, and keeps the wearer feeling dry even when damp. On its own silk has little elasticity, which makes it ideal for garments and accessories with drape. Silk is blended with other fibers in some wonderful yarns.

WOOL

Warm, durable, absorbs moisture and still keeps the skier feeling warm and dry, makes elastic fabric that fits well, is readily available, and the traditional fiber for so much skiwear. Everything to love for cold-weather knits! Wool felts beautifully; felted wool is even better than knitted fabric for blocking wind. Depending on the kind of sheep, wools vary in softness and elasticity. Some people are sensitive to wool next to their skin.

Merino wool, one of the softest available, is highly prized by outdoor athletes because it's excellent at regulating body temperature, providing warmth while wicking moisture away from the skin.

Superwash wool, which is treated to prevent felting during machine washing, is easier to care for than wool that requires hand-washing. Some Superwash wools can also be machine-dried.

BLENDS

Many yarns combine two or more fibers. Skilled yarn manufacturers choose and balance fibers for structure, appearance, easier care of finished garments, and affordability. Ball bands list the percentages of each fiber according to weight. A relatively light fiber like angora contributes substantial softness and warmth in blend where it has a small percentage of the weight. Silk may seem more prominent in volume than it is, because it is relatively heavy in weight. ❄

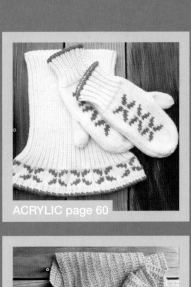
ACRYLIC page 60

ALPACA page 47

MOHAIR page 87

SILK page 26

WOOL page 129

SUPERWASH page 111

MERINO page 102

BLENDS page 50

❄ USEFUL INFORMATION

ABBREVIATIONS & TECHNIQUES

approx	approximately	M1 p-st	make 1 purl st	sssk	slip, slip, slip, knit (see glossary)
beg	begin(ning)	oz	ounce(s)	st(s)	stitch(es)
CC	contrasting color	p	purl	St st	stockinette stitch
ch	chain	pat(s)	pattern(s)	tbl	through back loop(s)
cm	centimeter(s)	pm	place marker		
cn	cable needle	psso	pass slip stitch(es) over	tog	together
cont	continu(e)(ing)			WS	wrong side(s)
dec	decreas(e)(ing)	rem	remain(s)(ing)	wyib	with yarn in back
dpn	double-pointed needle(s)	rep	repeat	wyif	with yarn in front
		RH	right-hand	yd	yard(s)
foll	follow(s)(ing)	RS	right side(s)	yo	yarn over needle
g	gram(s)	rnd(s)	round(s)	*	repeat directions following *
inc	increas(e)(ing)	SKP	slip 1, knit 1, pass slip st over (one st has been decreased)		
k	knit			[ ]	repeat directions inside brackets as many times as indicated
k2tog	knit 2 sts tog (one st has been decreased)				
		SK2P	slip 1, knit 2 tog, pass slip st over the knit 2 tog (two sts have been decreased)		
kfb	knit in front and back of next stitch to increase				
LH	left-hand	S2KP	slip 2 sts knitwise one at a time, knit 1, pass 2 slip sts over knit 1 (two sts have been decreased)		
lp(s)	loop(s)				
m	meter(s)				
mm	millimeter(s)				
MC	main color				
M1	make one st; with needle tip, lift strand between last st knit and next st on LH needle and knit into back of it	sl	slip		
		sl st	slip stitch		
		ssk	slip, slip, knit (see glossary)		

GAUGE

Make a test swatch at least 4"/10cm square. If the number of stitches and rows does not correspond to the gauge given, you must change the needle size. An easy rule to follow is: To get fewer stitches to the inch/cm, use a larger needle; to get more stitches to the inch/cm, use a smaller needle. Continue to try different needle sizes until you get the same number of stitches in the gauge.

Stitches measured over 4"/5cm.

Rows measured over 4"/5cm.

METRIC CONVERSIONS
To convert from inches to centimeters, simply multiply by 2.54.

SKILL LEVELS

◼◻◻◻ BEGINNER Ideal first project.

◼◼◻◻ EASY Basic stitches, minimal shaping and simple finishing.

◼◼◼◻ INTERMEDIATE For knitters with some experience. More intricate stitches, shaping and finishing.

◼◼◼◼ EXPERIENCED For knitters able to work patterns with complicated shaping and finishing.

GLOSSARY

bind off Used to finish an edge or segment. Lift the first stitch over the second, the second over the third, etc. (U.K.: cast off)

bind off in ribbing Work in ribbing as you bind off. (Knit the knit stitches, purl the purl stitches.) (U.K.: cast off in ribbing)

cast on Placing a foundation row of stitches upon the needle in order to begin knitting.

decrease Reduce the stitches in a row (that is, knit 2 together).

increase Add stitches in a row (that is, knit in front and back of stitch).

knitwise Insert the needle into the stitch as if you were going to knit it.

make one With the needle tip, lift the strand between the last stitch knit and the next stitch on the left-hand needle and knit into back of it. One knit stitch has been added.

make one p-st With the needle tip, lift the strand between the last stitch worked and the next stitch on the left-hand needle and purl into back of it. One purl stitch has been added.

no stitch On some charts, "no stitch" is indicated with shaded spaces where stitches have been decreased or not yet made. In such cases, work the stitches of the chart, skipping over the "no stitch" spaces.

place markers Place or attach a loop of contrast yarn or purchased stitch marker as indicated.

pick up and knit (purl) Knit (or purl) into the loops along an edge.

purlwise Insert the needle into the stitch as if you were going to purl it.

selvage stitch Edge stitch that helps make seaming easier.

slip, slip, knit Slip next two stitches knitwise, one at a time, to right-hand needle. Insert tip of left-hand needle into fronts of these stitches, from left to right. Knit them together. One stitch has been decreased.

slip, slip, slip, knit Slip next three stitches knitwise, one at a time, to right-hand needle. Insert tip of left-hand needle into fronts of these stitches, from left to right. Knit them together. Two stitches have been decreased.

slip stitch An unworked stitch made by passing a stitch from the left-hand to the right-hand needle as if to purl.

work even Continue in pattern without increasing or decreasing. (U.K.: work straight)

yarn over Making a new stitch by wrapping the yarn over the right-hand needle. (U.K.: yfwd, yon, yrn)

KNITTING NEEDLES

U.S.	Metric
0	2mm
1	2.25mm
2	2.75mm
3	3.25mm
4	3.5mm
5	3.75mm
6	4mm
7	4.5mm
8	5mm
9	5.5mm
10	6mm
10½	6.5mm
11	8mm
13	9mm
15	10mm
17	12.75mm
19	15mm
35	19mm

CROCHET HOOKS

U.S.	Metric
B/1	2.25mm
C/2	2.75mm
D/3	3.25mm
E/4	3.5mm
F/5	3.75mm
G/6	4mm
7	4.5mm
H/8	5mm
I/9	5.5mm
J/10	6mm
K/10½	6.5mm
L/11	8mm
M/13	9mm
N/15	10mm

☀USEFUL INFORMATION

STANDARD YARN WEIGHT SYSTEM

CATEGORIES OF YARN, GAUGE RANGES, AND RECOMMENDED NEEDLE AND HOOK SIZES

Yarn Weight Symbol & Category Names	**0** Lace	**1** Super Fine	**2** Fine	**3** Light	**4** Medium	**5** Bulky	**6** Super Bulky
Type of Yarns in Category	Fingering 10 count crochet thread	Sock, Fingering, Baby	Sport, Baby	DK, Light Worsted	Worsted, Afghan, Aran	Chunky, Craft, Rug	Bulky, Roving
Knit Gauge Range* in Stockinette Stitch to 4 inches	33 –40** sts	27–32 sts	23–26 sts	21–24 sts	16–20 sts	12–15 sts	6–11 sts
Recommended Needle in Metric Size Range	1.5–2.25 mm	2.25–3.25 mm	3.25–3.75 mm	3.75–4.5 mm	4.5–5.5 mm	5.5–8 mm	8 mm and larger
Recommended Needle U.S. Size Range	000 to 1	1 to 3	3 to 5	5 to 7	7 to 9	9 to 11	11 and larger
Crochet Gauge* Ranges in Single Crochet to 4 inch	32-42 double crochets**	21–32 sts	16–20 sts	12–17 sts	11–14 sts	8–11 sts	5–9 sts
Recommended Hook in Metric Size Range	Steel*** 1.6–1.4mm Regular hook 2.25 mm	2.25–3.5 mm	3.5–4.5 mm	4.5–5.5 mm	5.5–6.5 mm	6.5–9 mm	9 mm and larger
Recommended Hook U.S. Size Range	Steel*** 6, 7, 8 Regular hook B–1	B–1 to E–4	E–4 to 7	7 to I–9	I–9 to K–10½	K–10½ to M–13	M–13 and larger

* Guidelines only: The above reflect the most commonly used gauges and needle or hook sizes for specific yarn categories.

** Lace weight yarns are usually knitted or crocheted on larger needles and hooks to create lacy, openwork patterns. Accordingly, a gauge range is difficult to determine. Always follow the gauge stated in your pattern.

*** Steel crochet hooks are sized differently from regular hooks—the higher the number, the smaller the hook, which is the reverse of regular hook sizing.

BASIC STITCHES
Garter stitch
Knit every row.

Circular knitting
Knit one round, then purl one round.

Stockinette stitch
Knit right-side rows and purl wrong-side rows.

Circular knitting
Knit every round.

Reverse-stockinette stitch
Purl right-side rows and knit wrong-side rows.

Circular knitting
Purl every round.

Seed Stitch
Row 1 (RS) *Knit one, purl one; repeat from * to end.
Row 2 Knit the purl stitches and p the knit stitches.
Rep row 2 for seed stitch.

page 102

❋ESSENTIAL TECHNIQUES

LONG-TAIL CAST-ON

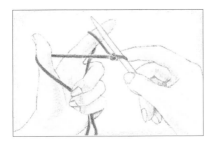

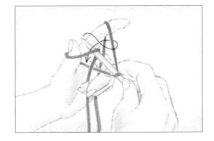

1. Make a slip knot on the right needle, leaving a long tail. Wind the tail end around your left thumb, front to back. Wrap the yarn from the ball over your left index finger and secure the ends in your palm.

2. Insert the needle upward in the loop on your thumb. Then with the needle, draw the yarn from the ball through the loop to form a stitch.

3. Take your thumb out of the loop and tighten the loop on the needle. Continue in this way until all the stitches are cast on.

KNIT-ON CAST-ON

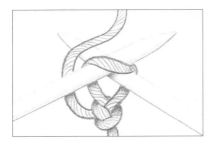

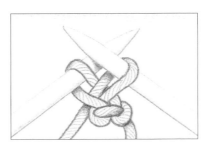

1. Make a slip knot on the left needle. *Insert the right needle knitwise into the stitch on the left needle. Wrap the yarn around the right needle as if to knit.

2. Draw the yarn through the first stitch to make a new stitch, but do not drop the stitch from the left needle.

3. Slip the new stitch to the left needle as shown. Repeat from the * until the required number of stitches is cast on.

CABLE CAST-ON

1. Cast on two stitches using the knit-on cast-on described above. *Insert the right needle between the two stitches on the left needle.

2. Wrap the yarn around the right needle as if to knit and pull the yarn through to make a new stitch.

3. Place the new stitch on the left needle as shown. Repeat from the *, always inserting the right needle in between the last two stitches on the left needle.

✳ESSENTIAL TECHNIQUES

KNITTING WITH CIRCULAR NEEDLES

Cast on as you would for straight knitting. Distribute the stitches evenly around the needle, being sure not to twist them. The last cast-on stitch is the last stitch of the round.
Place a marker here to indicate the end of the round.

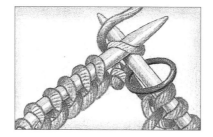

1 . Hold the needle tip with the last cast-on stitch in your right hand and the tip with the first cast-on stitch in your left hand. Knit the first cast-on stitch, pulling the yarn tight to avoid a gap.

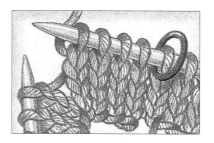

2 . Work until you reach the marker. This completes the first round. Slip the marker to the right needle and work the next round.

KNITTING WITH DPNS **Using Four Needles**

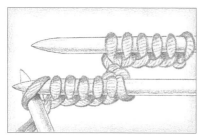

1. Cast on one third the required number of stitches on the first needle, plus one. Slip this extra stitch to the next needle as shown. Continue in this way, casting on the

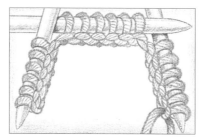

remaining stitches on the last needle.
2. Arrange the needles as shown, with the cast-on edge facing the center of the triangle.
3. Place a stitch marker after the last

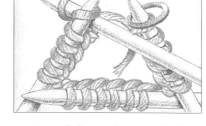

cast-on stitch, as shown, or in the first stich of the round. With the free needle, knit the first cast-on stitch, pulling the yarn tightly. Continue knitting in rounds, slipping the marker before beginning each round.

CABLES **Front (or Left) Cable**

1. Slip the first three stitches of the cable purlwise to a cable needle and hold them to the front of the work. Be careful not to twist the stitches.

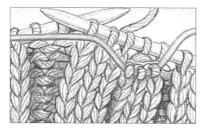

2. Leave the stitches suspended in front of the work, keeping them in the center of the cable needle where they won't slip off. Pull the yarn firmly and knit the next three stitches.

3. Knit the three stitches from the cable needle. If this seems too awkward, return the stitches to the left needle and then knit them.

Back (or Right) Cable

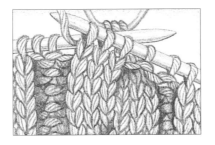

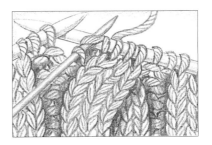

1. Slip the first three stitches of the cable purlwise to a cable needle and hold them to the back of the work. Be careful not to twist the stitches.

2. Leave the stitches suspended in back of the work, keeping them in the center of the cable needle where they won't slip off. Pull the yarn firmly and knit the next three stitches.

3. Knit the three stitches from the cable needle. If this seems too awkward, return the stitches to the left needle and then knit them.

FAIR ISLE STRANDING One-Handed

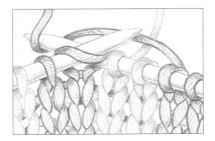

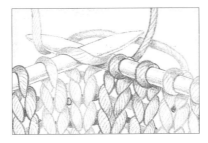

page 26

1. **On the knit side**, drop the working yarn. Bring the new color (now the working yarn) over the top of the dropped yarn and work to the next color change.

2. Drop the working yarn. Bring the new color under the dropped yarn and work to the next color change. Repeat steps 1 and 2.

page 91

1. **On the purl side**, drop the working yarn. Bring the new color (now the working yarn) over the top of the dropped yarn and work to the next color change.

2. Drop the working yarn. Bring the new color under the dropped yarn and work to the next color change. Repeat steps 1 and 2.

✳ESSENTIAL TECHNIQUES

INTARSIA Changing Colors on a Vertical Line

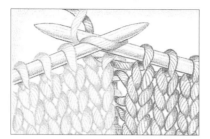

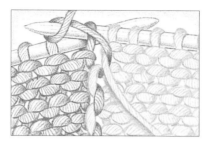

1. On the knit side, drop the old color. Pick up the new color from under the old color and knit to the next color change.

2. On the purl side, drop the old color. Pick up the new color from under the old color and purl to the next color change. Repeat steps 1 and 2.

page 29

Changing Colors on a Diagonal Line

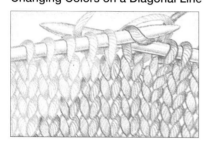

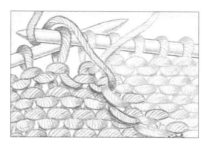

1. When working a right diagonal on the knit side, bring the new color over the top of the old color and knit to the next color change.

2. On the purl side, pick up the new color from under the old color and purl to the next color change.

page 66

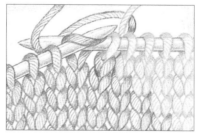

1. When working a left diagonal on the purl side, bring the new color over the top of the old color and purl to the next color change.

2. On the knit side, pick up the new color from under the old color and knit to the next color change.

KITCHENER STITCH (GRAFTING)

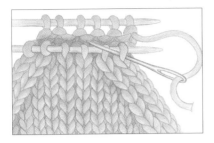

1. Insert tapestry needle purlwise (as shown) through first stitch on front needle. Pull yarn through, leaving that stitch on knitting needle.

2. Insert tapestry needle knitwise (as shown) through first stitch on back needle. Pull yarn through, leaving stitch on knitting needle.

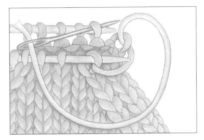

3. Insert tapestry needle knitwise through first stitch on front needle, slip stitch off needle and insert tapestry needle purlwise (as shown) through next stitch on front needle. Pull yarn through, leaving this stitch on needle.

4. Insert tapestry needle purlwise through first stitch on back needle. Slip stitch off needle and insert tapestry needle knitwise (as shown) through next stitch on back needle. Pull yarn through, leaving this stitch on needle.
Repeat steps 3 and 4 until all stitches on both front and back needles have been grafted. Fasten off and weave in end.

page 40

page 115

I-CORD

page 54

Cast on three to five sitches. *Knit one row. Without turning the work, slip the stitches back to the beginning of the row. Pull the yarn tightly from the end of the row. Repeat from the * as desired. Bind off.

❋ESSENTIAL TECHNIQUES

PICKING UP STITCHES ALONG A HORIZONTAL EDGE

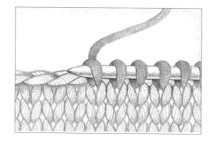

1. Insert the knitting needle into the center of the first stitch in the row below the bound-off edge. Wrap the yarn knitwise around the needle.

2. Draw the yarn through. You have picked up one stitch. Continue to pick up one stitch in each stitch along the bound-off edge.

PICKING UP STITCHES ALONG A VERTICAL EDGE

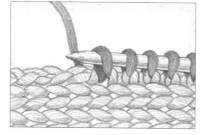

1. Insert the knitting needle into the corner stitch of the first row, one stitch in from the side edge. Wrap the yarn around the needle knitwise.

2. Draw the yarn through. You have picked up one stitch. Continue to pick up stitches along the edge. Occasionally skip one row to keep the edge from flaring.

PICKING UP STITCHES WITH A CROCHET HOOK

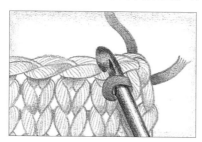

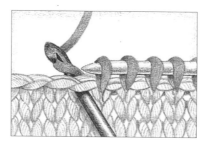

1. Insert the crochet hook from front to back into the center of the first stitch one row below the bound-off edge. Catch the yarn and pull a loop through.

2. Slip the loop onto the knitting needle, being sure it is not twisted. Continue to pick up one stitch in each stitch along the bound-off edge.

page 71

page 105

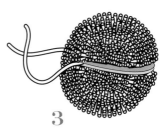

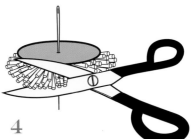

HOW TO MAKE A POMPOM

1. With two circular pieces of cardboard the width of the desired pompom, cut a center hole. Then cut a pie shaped wedge out of the circle. (Use the picture as a guide.)

2. Tightly hold the two circles together and wrap the yarn tightly around the cardboard. Then carefully cut around the cardboard.

3. Tie a piece of yarn tightly between the two circles. Remove the cardboard and trim the pompom.

4. Sandwich pompom between two round pieces of cardboard held together with a long needle. Cut around the circumference for a perfect pompom.

DUPLICATE STITCH

page 94

1. To cover a knit stitch in duplicate stitch, bring the needle up below the stitch to be worked.

2. Insert the needle under both loops one row above, and pull it through.

3. Insert it back into the stitch below and through the center of the next stitch in one motion.

EMBROIDERY

Chain Stitch
Draw the needle up and *insert it back where it just came out, taking a short stitch. With the needle above the yarn, hold the yarn with your thumb and draw it through. Repeat from *.

French Knot
Bring the needle up and wrap the thread around it once or twice, holding the thread taut. Reinsert the needle close to where the thread emerged.

✳ESSENTIAL TECHNIQUES

DOUBLE KNITTING

Double knitting is a method that creates double-sided fabric. Double-knit fabric may be created in either of two ways: by working a slip-stitch pattern that is identical on both sides or by knitting two fabrics at the same time with two yarns on one set of needles.

Double knitting can be done using straight, circular, or double-pointed needles. Because of its density, it uses twice as much yarn as single-face knitting. Double knitting creates a thick fabric suitable for blankets and outerwear. Though it shows as stockinette on both sides, the double thickness prevents the natural curling that would otherwise occur with stockinette stitch, creating nice flat hems and edgings on garments.

page 122

ZIPPERS

Whip stitch the zipper in place on the wrong side, then backstitch it on the right side close to the edge of the knit fabric.

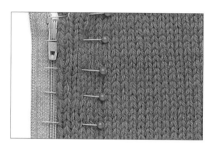

1. To apply the zipper, work from the right side of the piece or pieces with the zipper closed. Pin the zipper in place so that the edges of the knit fabric will cover the teeth of the zipper and meet in the center.

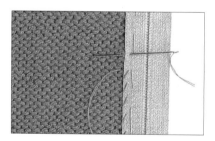

2. After pinning, baste the zipper and remove the pins. Turn the zipper to the wrong side and whip stitch in place. Turn the zipper to the right side and backstitch in place.

Open ended zipper

Closed ended zipper

❄ RESOURCES

STITCH MOUNTAIN
www.stitchmountain.com
Twitter: @stitchmountain

SKIING AND SNOWBOARDING
U.S. SKI AND SNOWBOARD ASSOCIATION
1 Victory Lane
Box 100
Park City, UT 84060
Tel: (435) 649-9090
ussa.org

YARNS
COATS & CLARK
CONSUMER SERVICES
P.O. Box 12229
Greenville, SC 29612-0229
www.coatsandclark.com

RED HEART
www.redheart.com

ROWAN
ROWAN
www.knitrowan.com

A MESSAGE FROM RED HEART® AND ROWAN®

We are proud to salute the U.S. skiers and snowboarders that inspire us all! The dedication and talents of the athletes profiled in this book have given us thrilling, proud moments in sports. Their stories of meaningful handknits are reminders to us of how magically a strand of yarn adds warm feelings and boosts confidence in the lives of those who have received lovingly made gifts.

Knitting with yarn is not only an outlet for creativity, but also a way to let others know we are rooting for them, whether they are competing as an athlete or facing any of life's challenges.

We hope the designs in this collection, knit with our Red Heart and Rowan brand yarns from the Coats Crafts family, provide enjoyment on your needles and, in turn, add warmth to the lives of many.

❋INDEX

※ADDITIONAL CREDITS

I'd like to acknowledge and thank these talented people, who helped us create our beautiful photos:

PHOTOGRAPHER'S ASSISTANT
Michael Okimoto

STYLIST'S ASSISTANT
Kaity Ocean

MAKEUP ASSISTANT
Laura Garcia

HAIR ASSISTANT
Keema Kelley

PRODUCTION ASSISTANT
Melinda McGinnis

MODELS
Rika Danko
Susie Knox
Emma McGinnis
Cassandra Walker
Annie Woods

A special thanks to these generous people and places for allowing us to shoot in their stunning locations:

Squaw Valley Ski Resort,
Olympic Valley, California

Olson Mountain Estate,
Martis Camp, California
ARCHITECT
Olson-Olson Architects
CONTRACTOR
Bruce Olson Construction

The neighborhood of Martis Camp,
California

✳ACKNOWLEDGMENTS

The concept for *Stitch Mountain* sat in the back of my mind for years, waiting for the right moment. I am sincerely grateful to the athletes, the designers, Red Heart, Rowan, Squaw Valley Ski Resort, and Jimmy Beans employees and customers for helping turn that concept into reality! Thanks to you, *Stitch Mountain* has been transformed from an off-the-wall idea into a unique and inspirational knitting book we can all be proud of.

Special thanks to the following, who were essential to the successful completion of *Stitch Mountain:*

EDIE THYS MORGAN
When Doug and I first met Edie—and presented this crazy idea—she jumped in to help. Right from the get-go she was contacting athletes and acting as a sounding board, and she even stepped in to write some text! Edie's enthusiasm for both knitting and skiing is infectious, and her energy was integral in making this book a reality. Always accessible and positive, Edie inspires me to be as selfless and gracious as she is. Edie, thank you for being a role model!

KIM BROWN
If we could have personal cheerleaders, Kim Brown would be mine. This book would never have happened without her. Kim's passion for snow sports and her enthusiastic support of Jimmy Beans and our unconventional foray into the world of skiing and snowboarding assuaged my doubts and fears about being outside my comfort zone. Kim, I know you get sick of my saying it, but you are my hero.

BRAD SWONETZ
Our photographer, a fellow knitter, and my new best friend. Brad, thank you for making our vision a reality. You truly are the best photographer on the planet and I'm honored to know you.

KAITY OCEAN AND MICHAEL FRANZESE
Without you, *Stitch Mountain* would not be what it is. You are a marketing dream team.

MY KNITTING DREAM TEAM
Sandy Hussey, Rachel Roden, Kristen Ashbaugh-Helmreich, Ellen Ashbaugh, and Debi Leonardini. Without you—and your late-night knitting—this book would have never happened.

SQUAW VALLEY
The most beautiful place on earth. Thanks to everyone at Squaw for being so supportive and providing access to the gorgeous scenery, and for introducing us to many of the athletes. Ski Squaw! Special thanks to Martis Camp in Truckee, for allowing us to photograph in their neighborhood, and to the Olson family for generously giving us access to the nicest house I've ever stepped foot in.

I would like to reiterate my appreciation of the athletes and designers for contributing their stories and creative energies to this book. Thank you so much for lending a piece of yourselves to this one-of-a-kind project that is so near and dear to my heart. ✳